PLAY WITH US

Play with Us is a selection of 100 games from all over the world. You will find games to play indoors or outdoors, to play on your own or to enjoy with a group. This book is the result of rigorous and detailed research done by the author over many years in the games' countries of origin. You might be surprised to discover where that game you like so much comes from or that at the other end of the world children play a game very similar to one you play with your friends. You will also have a chance to discover games that are unknown in your country but that you can have fun learning to play.

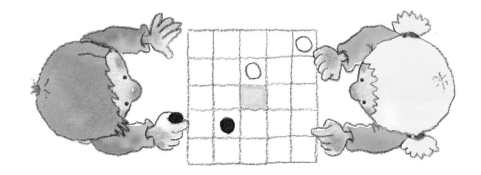

PLAY WITH US

100 Games from Around the World

Oriol Ripoll

CHICAGO
REVIEW
PRESS

Contents

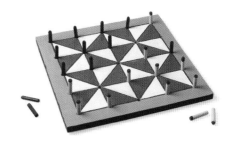

Playing traditional games gives people a way to gather, to communicate, and to express their ideas about themselves and their culture.

All the games listed here are identified by their countries of origin and are grouped according to similarities (game type, game pieces, game objective, etc.). Regardless of where they are played, games express the needs of people everywhere to move, think, and live together.

These games can be played by the whole family. They allow us to experience the concepts of space, time, gender, and other values common to the shared cultural heritage of humanity. This unique approach is a big reason why this collection exists!

A Game Box

Though some games require specific materials, most of what you need to play the games can be found wherever you live, around the world.

Baleros

These simple toys (usually made of wood) are a challenge to play alone or in competition with friends.

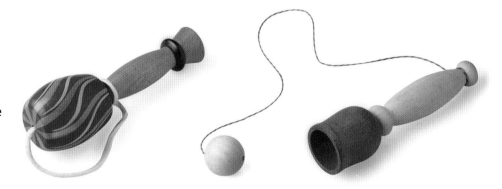

Quoits/Flat Pebbles

These objects are traditionally used in tossing games. You can use all kinds of flat objects such as stones, coins, seeds, pieces of wood or metal, or shoe heels. Beanbags or other small cloth bags stuffed with seeds may also be used as quoits.

Chalk

In many games it is necessary to mark the playing area with a starting and/or ending point or to draw a diagram to jump on or around. Depending on the surface, these markings can be made with a piece of chalk or a stick.

Dice

Dice may have two, four, six, or more faces, and they are often used to play traditional board games. A coin or a stick split in half can also make a good two-sided die. A die with four faces should be made from scratch.

Ball

Whether made of cloth or plastic, rubber or hide, the ball has been present in games played since ancient Roman, Greek, Mayan, and Aztec times.

Tops

Every country has its own version of a top. Some are made of clay, others of wood or stone. You can even make your own at home.

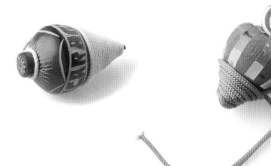

Marbles

Marbles are usually made of clay, glass, or steel, but sometimes you can even use dried fruit as marbles. Marbles, like many other objects used to play games, may also become collectors' pieces.

Pebbles, Bones, or Jacks

These small objects (often found in nature but are also sold in stores) are used to play a variety of games of skill or chance.

Cartetas

Cartetas can be made from old money, playing cards, or matchboxes.

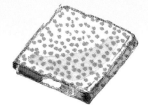

DO YOU KNOW HOW TO MAKE A *CARTETA*?

1–2. Divide a playing card in two approximately equal halves.

3. Arrange the two pieces so they form an L.

4–5–6. Fold the horizontal piece toward the back, then once more around to the front.

7. Fold the vertical piece forward just once.

8. Fold the vertical piece forward again so it will fit between the other two folds.

9. Cartetas show the card value on one side and the back of the card on the other side.

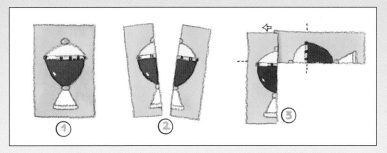

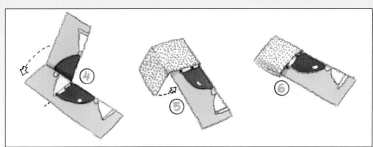

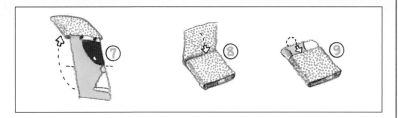

Boards for Games

Game boards can be made with simple materials; you can draw them on the ground or on a piece of wood. Some of the games included in this book require a playing board, and at the end of the book you will find different examples of boards that you can copy and then fasten to a hard surface.

Who Starts!

In many games, the players must decide who will be It, who will start the game, or what the order of the players will be. Making this decision can be a game in itself.

Manuhan

Philippines

- **Number of players:** 3 to 8
- **Material:** quoits for each player (a flat shoe heel, a flat pebble, or any other small, flat object)

1 Two parallel lines are drawn on the ground about 4 yards apart (the distance may be agreed on beforehand).

2 All players stand on one of the lines.

3 The players take turns throwing the shoe heel toward the opposite line.

4 The order in which players will play is determined by how close their heels land to the opposite line (closest goes first).

Zic, zac, zuc

Traditional game in Catalan-speaking areas
(Spain, France, Italy, and Andorra)

• **Number of players:** *more than 6*

1 All players stand in a circle with the tips of their right feet touching each other.

2 At the same time all the players say, "One, two, three, zic, zac, zuc, one, two, three."

3 Each player then either moves his or her foot outside the circle or keeps it where it is.

4 Whichever group—the players who moved their feet or the ones who didn't—is in the minority keeps playing, while the others are out. Repeat "one, two, three, zic, zac, zuc, one, two, three" with the remaining players.

5 The last player is It.

The Shoemaker

Mexico

• **Number of players:** *2*
• **Material:** *a pebble*

1 A player hides the pebble in one of his hands and makes two fists.

2 The player moves his fists up and down while saying, "Where does the shoemaker live, upstairs or downstairs?"

3 After the question, he places one fist on top of the other.

4 The second player guesses which fist holds the pebble and says "upstairs" or "downstairs."

5 The player with the pebble opens the indicated hand. If the pebble falls out, the player who guessed correctly is the winner. If the pebble does not fall out, the winner is the one holding the pebble.

DID YOU KNOW?
In Casablanca (Morocco), this game is played dropping the hand so it can be turned palm up or palm down. Before dropping the hand, the player says, "A la me set!"

Up or down

Pakistan

- **Number of players:** 3

1 All players stretch out their left hands with palms facing up.

2 When a sign is given, players put their right hands over their left hands, with the palms facing either up or down.

3 The winner is the player who places her hand in a position different from the other two.

Even or Odd

Catamarca, Argentina

- **Number of players:** 2
- **Material:** several small objects

1 One of the players hides a number of small objects in his closed hand and asks, "Even or odd?"

2 When the other player responds, the objects are counted to see if they are an even or an odd number.

DID YOU KNOW?

Another way to play this game is for both players to show several fingers at the same time while saying "Even or odd?" The winner is the player who guesses right.

Ram Ram Rip

Malaysia

- **Number of players:** 4 to 12

1 One of the players extends a hand with the palm facing up.

2 All the other players touch the palm of the hand with their index finger while saying, "Ram, ram, rip!"

3 As soon as the last word is pronounced, the first player closes her hand, trying to catch some of the fingers.

4 Whoever's finger is caught will be It.

5 If more than one finger is caught, repeat steps 2 and 3 but only with the players whose index fingers were caught.

Tick Tack

Scotland

• **Number of players:** 2

1 Players stand facing each other, about five yards apart.

2 Each player takes turns moving forward, placing one foot in front of the other so the heel touches the toe of the other foot.

3 When the players meet, the winner is the one who places his foot on top of the other player's foot.

Nawa Kuji

Japan

• **Number of players:** 4 to 8
• **Material:** a long piece of string

1 With a long length of string or thread, one player makes one loop in the string for each player.

2 The player holds the looped string in the fist of her left hand with the arches of the loops and the long end of the string hanging out of the top of her closed fist.

3 The player should hold the loops so no one can tell which loop is the first or last.

4 Each player puts his right index finger into one of the loops.

5 The player holding the string pulls the end of the string out of her fist. The first loop will tighten, and the player whose finger gets tied will be the first to start.

6 The player holding the string pulls it again (once for each remaining loop) to determine the order of participation for the rest of the players.

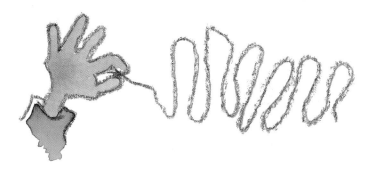

Guess with Your Senses!

It's fun to play games where we have to guess what's going on around us while we are blindfolded.

Draw the snake

Scotland

• **Number of players:** 4 to 12

1 One of the players is It and stands with his back to the other players.

2 The leader of the game draws the shape of a snake on the back of the player who is It and asks, "Who will draw the eye?"

3 One of the other players then goes up to It and touches his back with the tip of a finger (drawing the eye) and then goes back to stand with the other players.

4 The leader then tells It to turn around. It proposes a trick (for example, jumping like a frog all over the room) and then says the name of the player he thinks drew the eye of the snake on his back.

5 If It guesses right, the player who drew the eye has to perform the trick. That player then tries to tag the other players. The first player to be tagged becomes the new It.

6 If It does not guess right, he must perform the trick and continue being It for the next round of play.

Egg, Bell, Beak, or Spider?

(Huevo, Taña, Pico o Araña?)

Puerto Rico

• **Number of players:** *3 to 8*

2 One by one the players take turns getting on the donkey's back. With a finger, each player draws one of the shapes and asks the donkey, "Egg (*huevo*), bell (*taña*), beak (*pico*), or spider (*araña*)?"

3 If It guesses the shape right, the players switch positions.

1 The player chosen to be It gets on his hands and knees and pretends he is a donkey.

EGG

BELL

BEAK

SPIDER

Inelusul

Romania

• **Number of players:** *3 to 8*

1 The player who is It stands with her back to the other players.

2 The other players go near It and place a finger very close to It's back, but without touching her. The leader of the game tells one of the player to actually touch It's back with his finger.

3 Once It has been touched, all players go back to their places.

4 The game leader asks, "Whose finger touched you?"

5 The player who is It has to guess who touched her. If she guesses right, she switches roles. If not, she keeps being It.

The Alquerque and Its Variations

(The origin of this game is unknown, although many people believe it was first played in ancient Egypt. Different variations have developed all over the world since then.)

The Game of Alquerque

• **Number of players:** 2
• **Material:** *a game board (see the illustration below) and 24 playing pieces. Each player needs 12 pieces of one color.*

Step 1

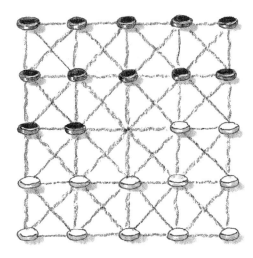

1 The playing pieces are placed on the board as shown in the illustration.

2 Each player takes a turn moving one of his or her playing pieces along a line to an empty position.

3 To capture an opponent's playing piece, you jump one of his pieces, but only if the position behind that playing piece is open. The playing piece that has been captured is removed from the board.

4 If it is your turn, and one of your opponent's playing pieces is open, you must jump and capture it. If you miss the chance to capture the opponent's playing piece, the piece is still taken off the board.

5 The same player may jump several playing pieces during one turn.

6 The winner is the player who is the first to capture all of her opponent's playing pieces.

DID YOU KNOW?
In Castile, King Alfonso X the Wise documented this game in a book. The game became very popular, and in Europe it was combined with the chessboard to create the game of checkers.

Step 2

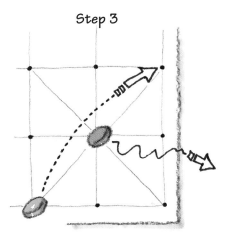

Step 3

Step 5

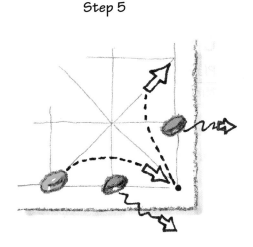

Kolowis Awithlaknannai

("Killing Stones")

Played by the Zuñi Indians in New Mexico

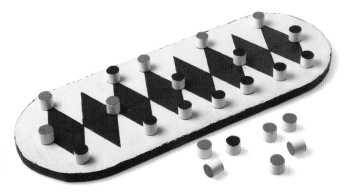

This version of the game requires each player to have 23 playing pieces of her own color. Use a game board that looks like the one shown below.

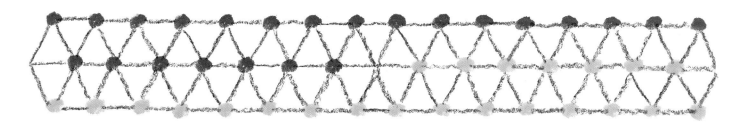

Terhuchu

Province of Assam, India

In this variation, a playing piece may be moved in a straight line to an open position inside the triangles. Each player starts by placing her nine pieces as shown in the illustration.

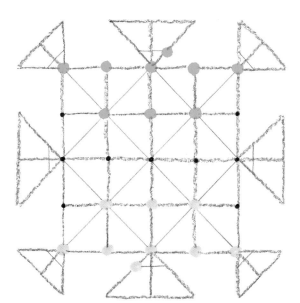

Chakka

Played by Bangladeshi people (in Bangladesh and the provinces of Calcutta and Assam in India)

Each player has only 6 pieces.

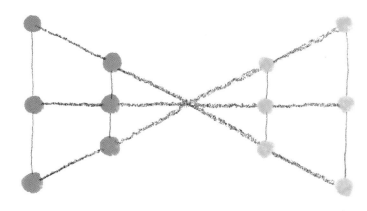

Backgammon

Variations on the game of backgammon can be found all over Asia, Africa, and Europe. The oldest boards date back to 3000 B.C.

Backgammon

Played in England

- **Number of players:** 2
- **Material:** a board, 2 dice, and 15 playing pieces of one color for each player

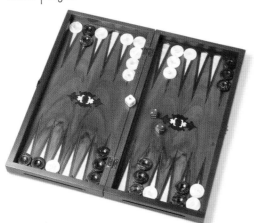

Step 1

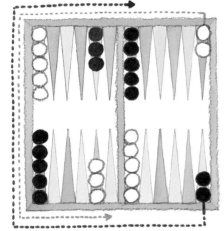

Step 2

1 The playing pieces are placed in their starting positions.

2 The object of the game is for each player to move his playing pieces to his own side of the board and then remove them from the board.

3 Each player takes turns throwing the dice. Playing pieces can be moved in the following ways:
- the face value of each individual die can be used to indicate the number of spaces two different playing pieces can move (A);
- the combined face value of both dice can be used to indicate the number of spaces one playing piece can move (B);
- if both dice show the same value, the player must use the combined value multiplied by two to move his playing pieces (C).

4 Based on the value shown on the upper face of the dice, the playing pieces may be moved in the following way:
- one playing piece moved to an empty position (A);
- a playing piece moved to a position occupied by one or more of the player's own playing pieces (B);
- a playing piece moved to a position occupied by one of the opponent's playing pieces in order to capture it (C);
- a playing piece may not be moved to a position occupied by more than one of the opponent's playing pieces (D).

BLACK PIECES

WHITE PIECES

5 When a playing piece is captured, it is placed over the central bar (A). The owner of this playing piece is not allowed to move any other playing pieces until the captured piece is put back into play on the board (B).

6 Once a player has moved all his playing pieces to his own side of the board, he tries to remove them from the board following the value of the dice thrown. Removing the playing pieces from the board does not require an exact throw of the dice.

7 The winner is the player who removes all his playing pieces from the board first.

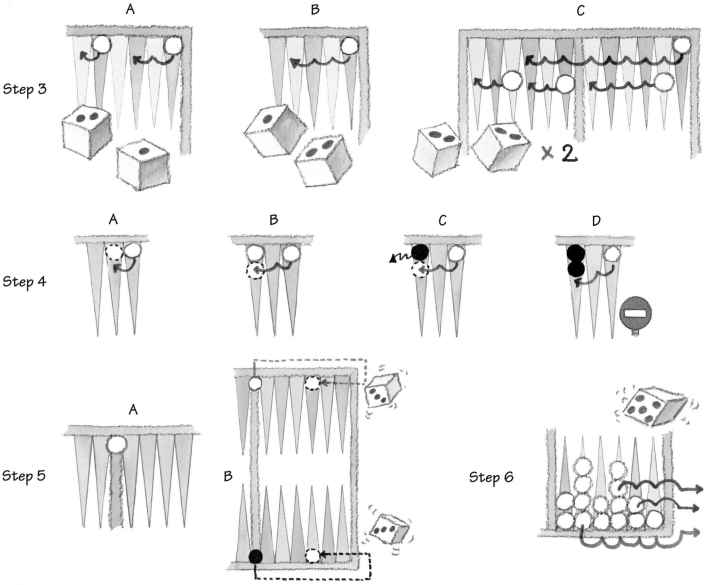

Step 3   A   B   C   × 2

Step 4   A   B   C   D

Step 5   A   B   Step 6

Betting

Before the game starts, the players agree on the amount of the bet.

A player may double her bet during the game when it is her turn—but only before throwing the dice. Once the bet has been doubled, only the opponent has the right to double it again.

If a player refuses to double the bet, she loses the game and must pay the amount previously agreed.

Bets are paid in the following way:

- The loser pays the agreed bet if she succeeds in removing at least one playing piece from the board.
- If the loser cannot remove any of her playing pieces from the board, she pays double the agreed amount.
- This is called a gammon.
- If the loser cannot remove any of her playing pieces from the board, and if, in addition, some of her playing pieces remain on the central bar or in the opponent's side of the board, she has to pay three times the agreed amount. This is called backgammon.

To mark the bets, players may use a special die called the doubling cube with the values 2, 4, 8, 16, 32, and 64 marked on it.

Tabula

First century A.D. Rome

- **Number of players:** 2
- **Material:** *a board, 3 dice, and 15 playing pieces for each player*

1 The game starts with an empty board.

Putting the playing pieces onto the board

2 In the first phase of the game, the playing pieces must be put on the board. To do so, the three dice are thrown, and one, two, or three playing pieces enter the board (each according to the face value of the individual die, or one according to the combined face value of all three dice).

3 If the faces of the three dice show the same value, the first 12 positions cannot hold more than one playing piece of the same color.

Movement of the playing pieces

4 When all the playing pieces are on the board, they are moved counterclockwise around the board, toward the finish line.

5 To move a playing piece, the player throws the three dice. These may be used separately for moving individual pieces or together by adding the values for one solo move.

6 A playing piece may not be moved to a position occupied by more than one of the opponent's playing pieces.

7 If a playing piece ends up in a position occupied by more than one of the opponent's playing pieces, it is captured. More than one playing piece may be captured in the same move. A captured playing piece is removed from the board and the owner is forced to bring it back during her next move.

8 Entering the board and capturing a playing piece may be done at the same time.

9 When all the playing pieces are between positions 19 and 24, players may start removing them from the board.

10 The winner is the player who removes all of her playing pieces from the board first.

DID YOU KNOW?

This illustration shows the famous hand of the Roman emperor Zenon, who played with white pieces and drew a 2, a 5, and a 6. He was forced to leave pieces without protection all over the board.

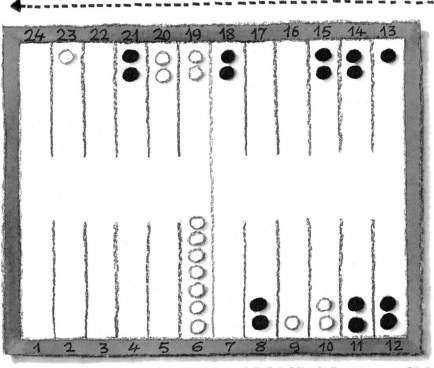

Caixó

Island of Minorca, Spain

• **Number of players:** 2
• **Material:** *a board, 3 dice, and 15 playing pieces for each player*

1 The playing pieces are placed as shown in the illustration.

2 The aim is to remove all the playing pieces from the board.

3 Each player takes turns throwing the dice, and moves one, two, or three playing pieces.

4 If two of the values are the same, both dice are counted as if they were four. If three of the values are the same, it is *bacarral*, and the three dice are counted as if they were six and the player gets to throw the dice again.

5 In this version of the game, the players do not capture the opponent's playing pieces.

6 A playing piece may not be placed on a space occupied by an opponent's playing piece.

7 If the values on the thrown dice can't be used by the player who threw them, the opponent may use them in his or her next turn.

8 While all the pieces are still in the first quarter of the board, there may not be more than two positions occupied by one player's pieces of the same color.

9 The playing pieces are removed from the board following the same rules used in backgammon (see pages 18–19).

10 The game is usually played to the best of five rounds.

Step 1

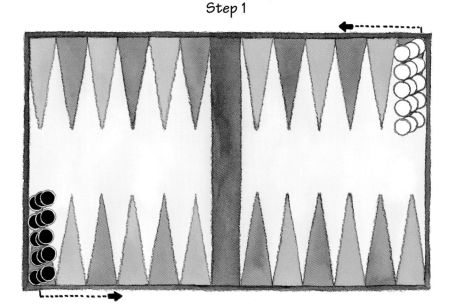

Step 4

When the value of the three dice is the same, it is bacarral.

Step 6

Step 8

Games of Solitaire

Many new versions of solitaire are now being created because, within the family of board games, there have only been a few throughout history that have been traditionally played by only one person.

Ise-ozin-egbe

("Patience")

Nigeria

• **Material:** *26 seeds on a board that has 6 pits*

Step 1

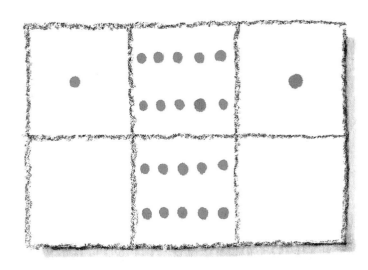

1 The seeds are placed on the board as shown in the illustration.

2 The game begins by taking all the seeds from the central pit in the upper row and sowing them clockwise.

3 The last seed always falls in an occupied pit, where all the seeds are collected again and the sowing begins again.

4 If the sowing is done correctly, the starting formation will be made again after 144 moves.

Step 2

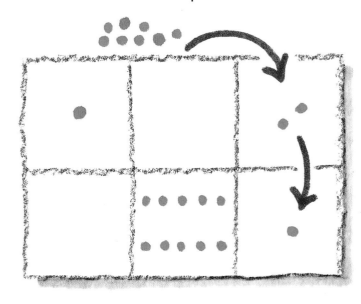

DID YOU KNOW?

Like most of the games from the mancala family (see page 100), Ise-ozin-egbe is usually played by making holes in the ground. The game is meant to be played to practice the skills needed for sowing.

French and English Solitaire

Probably invented in France sometime in
the 18th century

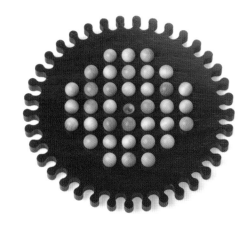

According to legend, this game was invented by a no-
bleman jailed in the Bastille during the 18th century.
The game can be played in two different ways:
• English solitaire is played with 32 playing pieces on a
  33-hole board.
• French solitaire is played with 36 playing pieces on a
  37-hole board.

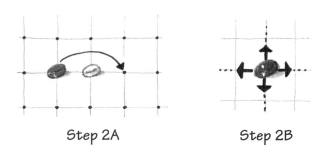

Step 2A   Step 2B

1 The playing pieces are placed in all the holes except
the central one.

2 The playing pieces are moved by jumping over
another playing piece (A) to an unoccupied hole.
Playing pieces can only be moved forward, backward,
or sideways, never diagonally (B).

3 The game is over when there is only one playing
piece left on the board.

Tchuka Ruma

Eastern India

1 The pieces are placed in the starting position.

2 The player collects all the playing pieces from one
of the holes and sows them clockwise from left to
right.

3 When the player arrives at the largest hole (the
ruma) and still has seeds in his hand, she continues
sowing to the left.

4 If the sowing ends in the ruma, the player chooses
where she wants to start sowing in the next round.

5 The game is finished when all the seeds are in the
ruma.

6 If the game finishes in an empty hole, the player
loses the game.

*There are different
versions in which
the holes are distrib-
uted in circles. In the
commercial version
shown here, the
game is played with
rings instead of
seeds.*

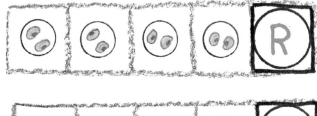

Surprise Chase

All the games in this section have one common feature: a player must chase the others who don't know when they have to start running. These games call for agility and speed.

Moto kumapiri

("Fire in the Mountain")

Malawi

- **Number of players:** more than 10

1 Choose a player to be It.

2 The rest of the group stands in pairs forming two circles. One member of each pair stands forming an inner circle while the other members of the pairs form an outer circle.

3 The players start moving clockwise as they sing "*moto kumapiri*" ("fire in the mountain").

4 When It shouts "*Wazima!*" ("the fire has been lit"), It and the rest of the players try to climb on the back of any player in the inner circle.

5 The player without a partner will be It in the next round.

Da ga

("Boa Constrictor")

Ghana

• **Number of players:** more than 6

1 An area is marked on the ground: it is the snake's house. The player who is the snake stands inside the snake's house. The rest of the players scatter around the playing area and call to the snake.

2 When the snake decides, it runs out of its house trying to catch the players. When a player is caught, both the snake and the player who was caught go back to the snake's house.

3 When there are two or more playing the part of the snake, they must hold hands and form a chain while chasing the other players.

4 If the chain is broken while chasing the other players, they must go back to the snake's house.

The Honeycomb

El Salvador

• **Number of players:** more than 6
• **Material:** any object (it may be a ball)

1 Choose who will be It. The rest of players hold hands and form a spiral (the honeycomb).

2 The player who is It holds the object and walks around the honeycomb while saying "home" to the other players.

3 When It decides, he tosses the object toward the honeycomb. The players forming the honeycomb separate to chase after It, trying to tag him.

4 The first player to tag It will switch positions and will be the new It in the next round of the game.

No One Left

Every board games in this section has the same objective: to capture all the opponent's playing pieces.

Step 1

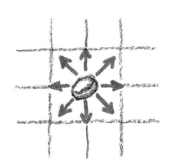

Surakarta

Island of Java

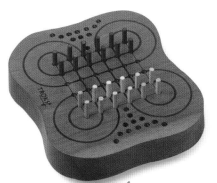

- **Number of players:** 2
- **Material:** a board and 12 playing pieces per player

1 Each player moves one of his playing pieces when it is his turn.

2 There are two kinds of moves:
- When it is not going to capture another playing piece, the playing piece may be moved to any unoccupied position next to it.
- To capture an opponent's playing piece, a player must move a playing piece along the line where it is located, go into one of the circles, stop at the opponent's playing piece, and remove it from the board. To make this move, the path must be completely free of other playing pieces. The capturing playing piece may have to go into more than one circle. A playing piece may go into only one circle to capture another playing piece.

3 The winner is the player who captures all his opponent's playing pieces.

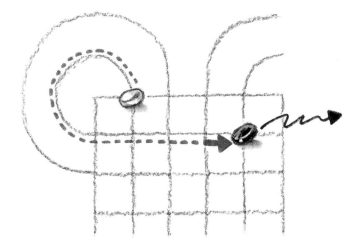

Step 2

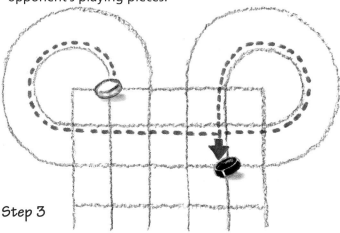

Step 3

DID YOU KNOW?

This game is traditionally played on a board drawn on the ground and uses snails and pebbles as playing pieces. At the end of the 20th century, it was named after an important city on the island of Java because until then it was known only as "the game."

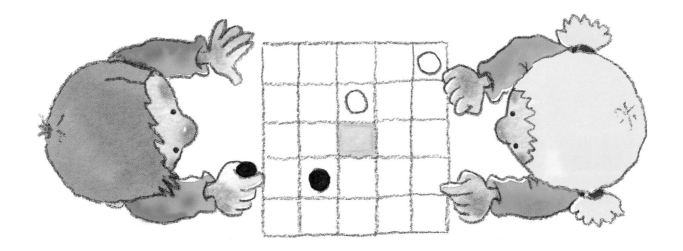

Sija

Played by the Fellahin and Somali peoples in Sudan, Egypt, and Somalia

• **Number of players:** 2
• **Material:** a board and 12 playing pieces for each player

The board is empty when the game starts.

Placing the playing pieces on the board

1 Decide who will place his playing pieces on the board first. Each player takes a turn, placing two playing pieces in unoccupied positions. Until all pieces have been placed on the board, the middle position must remain unoccupied.

Moves and capturing

2 The last player to put his final playing pieces on the board is the one who moves first. If he cannot make a move, he removes one of the opponent's playing pieces from the board and loses his turn.

3 A playing piece may move to any unoccupied position, including the one in the middle.

4 If an opponent's playing piece ends up between two of the current player's playing pieces, that playing piece is captured and removed from the board. A player must continue moving and capturing all of the opponent's playing pieces possible during one turn.

Step 3

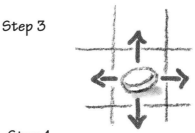

Step 4

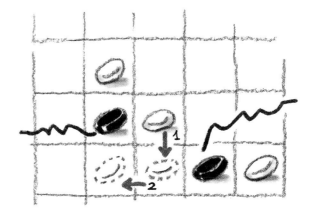

5 It is mandatory to capture a playing piece, if possible.

6 A playing piece occupying the central position cannot be captured.

7 The winner is the player who captures all of his opponent's playing pieces or who has no further moves available.

Games of Tag

The common feature of these games is the safe place where players cannot be touched by the chaser.

Ka fao jai

("Mother Raven's Eggs")

Thailand

- **Number of players:** 4 to 10
- **Material:** 10 pebbles representing eggs and something to mark the ground (such as a piece of chalk)

A circle about 3 feet (1 m) wide is drawn on the ground. It is the raven's nest. The 10 eggs are placed inside the nest. A player is chosen to be the Mother Raven, and this player steps into the nest. The game is played in three stages.

Stage one:

1 The game starts when one of the players says, "Defend your eggs."

2 The players outside the circle try to grab the eggs, but the Mother Raven defends them with her hands and feet while trying to tag one of the thieves.

3 The first player who is tagged by the Mother Raven is out. The game starts again and the player who was tagged is now the Mother Raven.

Stage two:

If the thieves are able to snatch away all the eggs from the nest without being tagged by the Mother Raven, the second stage of the game starts.

1 The Mother Raven is blindfolded.

2 While the Mother Raven is blindfolded, the eggs are hidden. The Mother Raven has three opportunities to find her eggs. If she can't, she is shown where they were hidden.

Stage three:

1 When the Mother Raven finds an egg, she picks it up and tries to tag one of the thieves with it. The player who is tagged becomes the new Mother Raven.

2 If no player is tagged, the Mother Raven keeps being It and the game starts again.

Tih

Morocco

- **Number of players:** 4 to 10
- **Material:** a sneaker for each player and one walking stick

1 A circle about 6 feet (2 m) in diameter is drawn on the ground. All the sneakers are placed inside the circle.

2 A player is chosen to be It and stands in the middle of the circle holding the walking stick to the ground.

3 When the signal is given, the players try to kick their sneakers out of the circle using their feet. It tries to tag the players with her feet but must hold onto the walking stick at all times.

4 If It tags one of the players, they switch roles.

5 If the players in the outside circle get all the sneakers without being touched, It starts running. The other players chase It and try to tag her with a sneaker. When one of the players tags It, the game starts again.

The Guardian of the Good Cabbage

Described with different names in several areas in Spain and France

- **Number of players:** 4 to 10
- **Material:** a long rope (between 3 [1 m] and 15 feet [3 m] long)

1 A player is chosen to be the cabbage. He sits on the ground and holds one end of the rope. Another player holds the other end of the rope and is the guardian of the cabbage.

2 The other players try to touch the cabbage without being tagged by the guardian.

3 When the guardian tags a player, the player becomes the cabbage. The player who was the previous cabbage becomes the guardian, and the previous guardian becomes a player trying to touch the cabbage.

Tolchi Nori

This game of skill and aim is traditionally played by girls. It is usually divided into 18 games. After number 12, some positions are repeated, by jumping backward.

Tolchi Nori

Korea

- **Number of players:** 4 to 8 divided into 2 teams
- **Material:** one pebble (or shoe heel) for each player

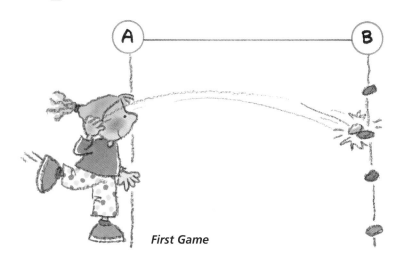

First Game

Second Game

Basic rules

1 Two parallel lines are drawn on the ground, about 8 feet (2.5 m) apart.

2 Tolchi is a series of 18 games. The first team to complete the entire series wins.

3 When one of the players in a team fails one of the series, her team loses its turn. When the team starts playing again, the players pick up the game where they left off.

First game

1 All the players on the throwing team (A) stand behind the line.

2 The players on the other team (B) place their pebbles on the opposite line.

3 Each player on the throwing team chooses a pebble belonging to the other team. When it is her turn, she throws her pebble, trying to hit the chosen one on the opposite line.

4 If all the players hit their targets, they go on to the second game. If any of the players fail, the opposing team plays.

Second game

1 All the players on the throwing team throw their pebbles to a distance they can reach with one jump.

2 From the throwing line, each player must jump and land with one foot on her pebble.

3 Leaning on her heel, the player lifts her foot off the pebble, picks it up, and throws it trying to hit a chosen pebble belonging to the opposite team.

4 The player cannot touch the ground with her other foot at any time.

Third game

Fifth game: Place the pebble on the instep.

Sixth game: The pebble is held between both feet.

Seventh game: The pebble is held between the knees.

Eighth game: The pebble is held between the thighs.

Fourth game

Ninth game: The player leans backward and places the pebble on her chest.

Third game
This is played like the second game, except that the pebble is thrown to a distance that can be reached in two jumps.

Fourth game
Played like the second game, but the player has to reach the pebble in three jumps.

Fifth game

1 The players on the throwing team place their pebbles on the instep of their feet and jump forward as many times as they wish.

2 When they are close to the opposite line, they throw their pebbles, trying to hit the opponent's chosen pebble.

3 If the pebble falls off the instep or the player fails her throw, she loses her turn.

The sixth through the twelfth games are played the same way but change the place on the body where the pebble carried.

Tenth game: The pebble is carried over the left shoulder.

Eleventh game: The pebble is carried over the right shoulder.

Twelfth game: The pebble is held between the chin and the neck.

Games of Strength

These team games can be as friendly or as competitive as you'd like.

Haneqe

("Tied Hand," or Shedat in Arabic)

Played by the Nubian people in northern Sudan and southern Egypt

• **Number of players:** 2 teams with 4 to 8 members each

• **Material:** a piece of chalk or a stick to draw on the ground

1 Form two teams. One will attack, and the other will defend.

2 Draw a circle on the ground.

3 All players hop on one leg while holding the other leg with his or her hand.

4 The attack team chooses one of the players to be It. His teammates try to help him enter the circle.

5 The defending team will try to prevent It from getting into the circle by blocking the way.

6 All players from both teams will try to make the opponents touch the ground with both feet. If a player's other foot touches the ground, he or she is eliminated.

7 If the attack team reaches its target, they attack again. If not, they switch roles and the other team attacks.

Chak-ka-yer

Thailand

- **Number of players:** *more than 6*
- **Material:** *a piece of chalk to draw a line on the ground*

1 Form two teams. One team is the good ghosts and the other team the bad ghosts.

2 A line is drawn on the ground and both teams stand on either side.

DID YOU KNOW?

This game, described by children in northern Thailand, may also be played by eliminating players: when a player is dragged over the other side, she is out of the game.

3 At the starting signal, the players in both teams will try to grab an opponent and drag her over the line to the other side.

4 The players on the team of the good ghosts may form a chain to help one another.

5 The players on the team of the bad ghosts may only drag the players from the other team individually, without any help.

6 When a player is dragged over the line, she becomes a member of the opposite team.

7 The game is over when all the players are on one side of the line.

Checkers

Checkers is actually a variation of the old game of alquerque (see page 16) and was very popular in medieval Europe. The variations of this game include a variety of moves, playing pieces, and/or the number of squares on the checkerboard.

English checkers

- **Number of players:** 2
- **Material:** a checkerboard of 8 squares by 8 squares, 11 playing pieces or checkers per player

The checkerboard is placed so the bottom right square is always white.

DID YOU KNOW?

There are two rules traditionally used that are not part of the official rules of this game:
- When a checker is able to capture an opponent's checker but does not do so, it is "blown" (removed from the checkerboard).
- The queen may be moved as many squares as the player wishes. When the queen captures a checker, she must occupy the square next to the one previously occupied by the captured checker.

1 The game starts with a move from a white checker. The piece must be moved diagonally into an empty square.

2 A checker can capture another by jumping over it and landing on an empty square on the other side of it. You have to capture whenever possible.

3 Two or more captures can be made in one move.

4 When one of the checkers gets to the back row on the other end of the board, it is crowned with another checker of the same color on top (A). This becomes the queen. The queen can move diagonally, forward, or backward (B).

5 Any checker may capture the queen.

6 The winner is the player who captures all of the opponent's checkers.

Step 1

Step 2

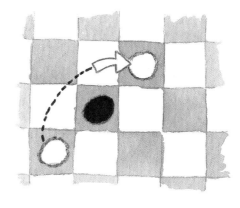

Step 3

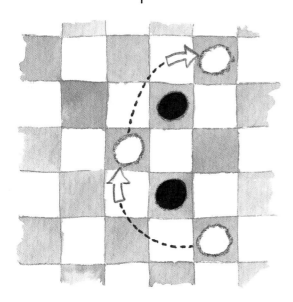

QUEEN

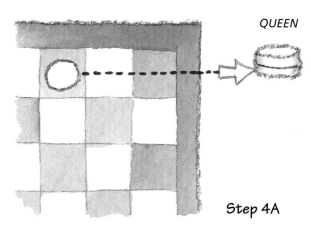

Step 4A

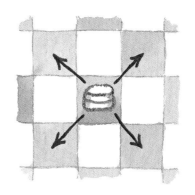

Step 4B

Atlanbaj

(Turkish Checkers)

Played in Eastern Europe

Number of players: 2

Material: a checkerboard of 8 squares by 8 squares and 16 pieces per player

1 Each player, in turn, moves a checker either forward or sideways. No diagonal or backward moves are allowed.

2 When a checker gets to the last square, it is crowned as king.

3 To distinguish the king from the other checkers, another checker of the same color is placed on top. The king may move forward, backward, or sideways as many squares as the player wishes in one turn.

4 One checker can capture another by jumping over it to an unoccupied square next to it. The captures may be double or triple.

5 The winner is the first player to capture all of the opponent's checkers.

Step 1

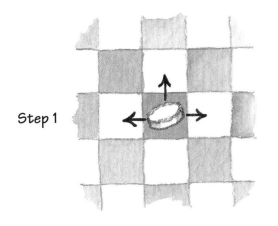

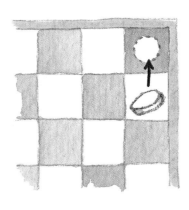

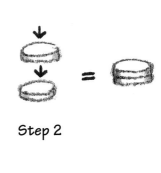

Step 2

Step 3

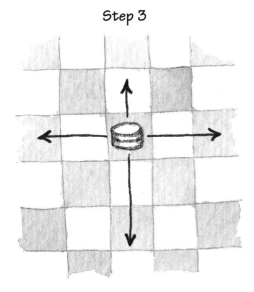

Step 4

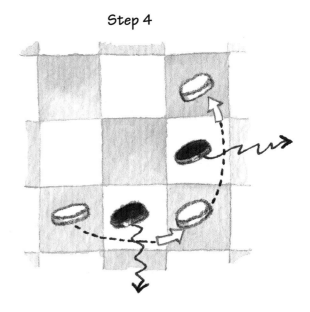

Belgian checkers

(Losing Is Winning)

France and England

This game is played with the same rules as English checkers with one difference: the winner is the player to lose all her checkers!

Italian checkers

Played in Italy at the end of the 16th century

This game is played with the same rules as English checkers, with one difference: the queens can only be eliminated by other queens. A player must capture his opponent's checkers. If he doesn't, he loses the game.

If a player has a choice between two moves, he must choose the one allowing him the most captures. If both options have the same number of pieces to capture, the player must capture the ones with the higher value.

Shashki

(Russian checkers)

Played in Russia and Eastern European countries

Checkers can only move forward, although they may move backward to capture. The queen may move forward or backward as many squares as the player wishes.

DID YOU KNOW?

Polish checkers are played on a checkerboard of 10 squares by 10 squares and 20 checkers per player.
Canadian checkers are played on an even larger checkerboard of 12 squares by 12 squares, and 30 checkers per player.

Skelly

(The players try to get a bottle cap onto a central square and then back again to the starting line. The squares are numbered and must be played in sequence.)

Skelly

Played in the streets of New York City

• **Number of players:** 2 to 6
• **Materials:** bottle caps (metal or plastic) or coins pressed into clay or beeswax and a piece of chalk

The size and number of squares depend on the number of players and how long the game will last. The large play square, which can be as small as 3 feet (1 m) or as large as 6 feet (2 m), is drawn on the ground with chalk.

How to play

1 The players decide the order in which they will play. All players place their bottle caps on the starting line.

2 The players take turns flicking their bottle caps with their fingers to move them from box to box, in numerical order.

3 On the first turn, all players try to flick their bottle caps into box number one.

4 When a player makes the bottle cap land in the right box, she gets another turn.

5 If the bottle cap does not land in the box, it stays where it lands until the player's next turn.

6 When a player hits another player's bottle cap, her piece moves directly to the next box, and she gets an extra turn.

7 The box in the center is surrounded by other boxes with skulls, or other "danger" signs, drawn in them. If a bottle cap lands on one of the boxes marked with a skull, the player loses three turns.

8 As soon as a player's piece has gone through all the boxes in the proper order and has reached the center box, the player has to move his piece back to the starting line, following the same rules and landing on all the numbered boxes in reverse order.

9 Any bottle cap that makes it back to the starting line becomes a "poisoned cap." If a poisoned cap touches another cap, the other cap is eliminated from the game.

10 Players who have poisoned caps no longer have to go through the boxes in order; she just tries to hit other bottle caps with her poisoned caps to eliminate them.

11 The player with the last bottle cap remaining in the game is the winner.

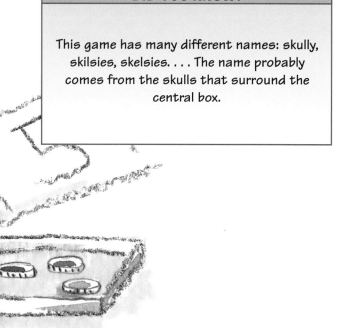

DID YOU KNOW?

This game has many different names: skully, skilsies, skelsies. . . . The name probably comes from the skulls that surround the central box.

Blocking Games

In the games in this section, players try to stop their opponents from moving.

Konane

Hawaii

- **Number of players:** 2
- **Material:** a board of 10 boxes by 10 boxes, 50 pieces per player.

1 The player moving the white pieces removes one from the board. This piece should be removed from one of the corners or from the center of the board.

2 The player moving the black pieces removes one of his pieces from the side of the empty space left by the white piece. If the white piece was removed from the center, then the black piece must be taken from a center box.

3 Each player takes turns jumping one of his opponent's pieces and moves his piece to an empty box. The player can make more than one jump as long as it's in the same direction.

4 The player who cannot make any further moves or does not have any more pieces loses the game.

Step 1

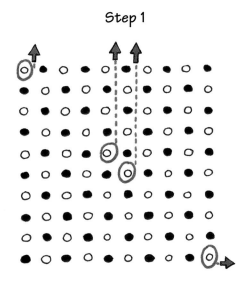

Step 3

Yagua

Played by the Chiriguano-chané people in Argentina.
Also played by the Araucanian people in Chile.

Number of players: 2
Material: a board (usually drawn on the ground),
12 pebbles or seeds representing the dogs, and a
different one representing the jaguar

*The illustration represents
the starting positions.*

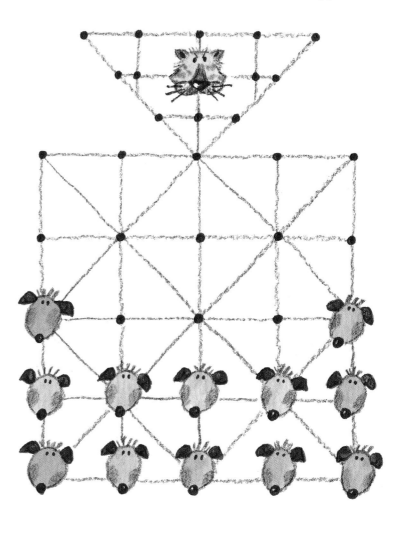

1 One of the players moves the jaguar (yagua)
and the other moves the dogs (the yamba).

2 The jaguar moves first.

3 The jaguar wins the game if it "eats" all the
dogs (by jumping and capturing them). As soon
as the jaguar is able to eat at least three dogs, it
wins because there are no longer enough dogs
to successfully corner the jaguar.

4 The dogs win if they corner the jaguar so it
can make no further moves.

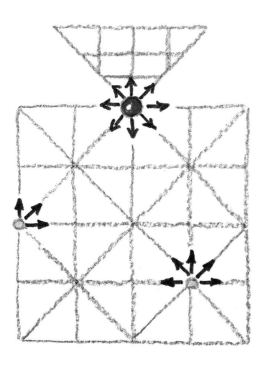

*The jaguar can move
in any direction. The
dogs cannot move
backward.*

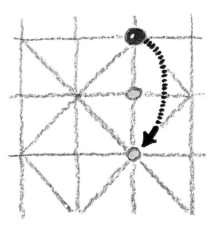

*The jaguar can capture a
dog by jumping over an-
other dog.*

Bagh chal

("Move the Tigers")

Nepal

- **Number of players:** 2
- **Material:** *a game board, 4 pieces (tigers) for one of the players and 20 pieces (sheep) for the other*

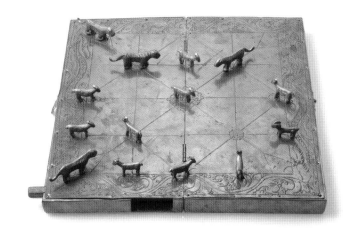

1 The player moving the tigers places them at the four corners of the board. The sheep start the game from outside the board.

2 The players take turns making a move:
- the player with the sheep places one sheep in an unoccupied position;
- the player with the tigers may move any piece.

3 The tigers eat the sheep by jumping over one of them to an empty position.

4 The sheep, in turn, try to keep the tigers from moving. If they succeed, they win.

5 The tigers win if they can capture five sheep.

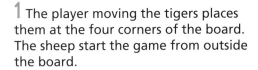

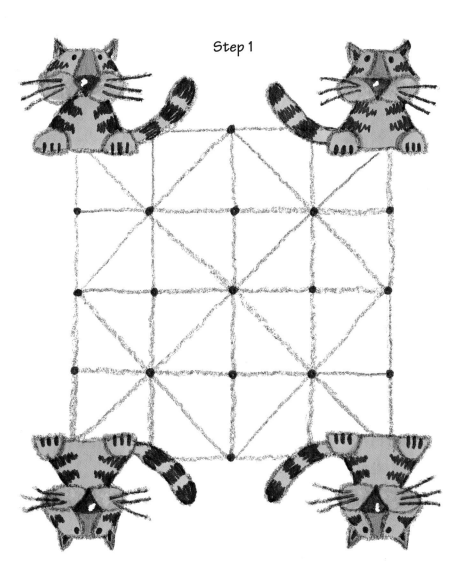

The tigers are originally placed at the four corners of the board.

Step 2

The tiger can move in any direction to an unoccupied position.

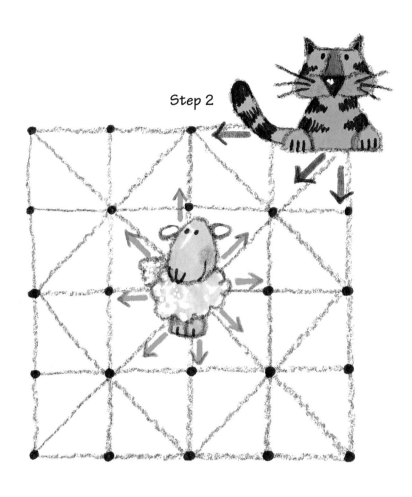

Step 3

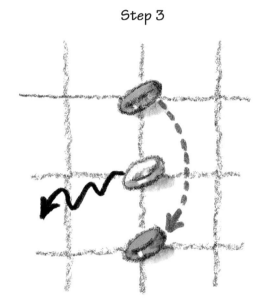

Step 4

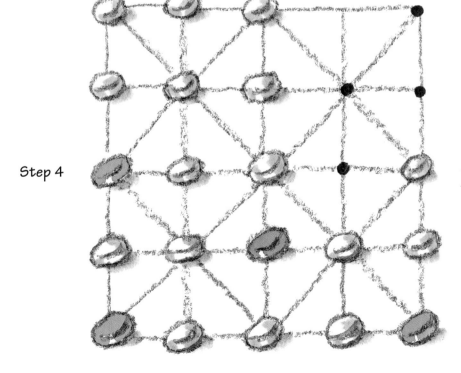

The tigers can't move because they are surrounded by sheep.

The Assault

Played in many European countries

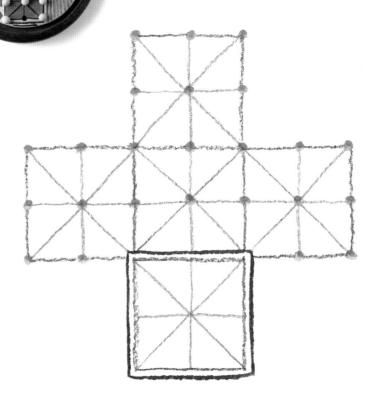

During a certain period of time in England, this game was called "Officers and Sepoys," after a revolt of Hindu troops in 1875.

This game is played following the same rules as Yagua. The defenders of the fortress try to eliminate the attackers, while the attackers try to occupy the nine positions that form the fortress.

Fox and Geese

Played throughout Europe

This game is described in an Icelandic book written around 1300. The game was also found described in a book from around 1283, during the reign of King Alfonso X of Castile, under the name of *"Cercar la liebre"* ("Corner the Hare"). It was played on an alquerque board.

This game is played following the same rules as Yagua. One of the players moves the fox and the other player moves the geese. The geese try to corner the fox so he can't move before he eats them all.

The three possible starting positions for Fox and Geese

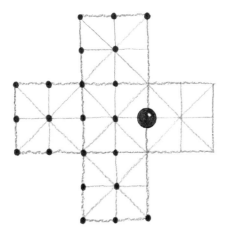
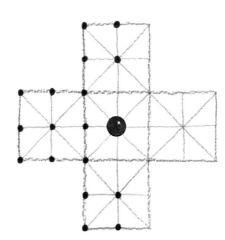
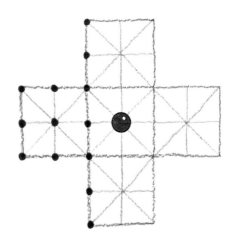

Uxrijn Ever

("The Ox Horn")

**Played by the children of the Mongolian People's
Republic, parts of China, and other Asian republics**

- **Number of players:** 2
- **Material:** a board, 2 pieces (cowboys) for one
player, and 2 pieces (a cow and a calf) for the other
player

Knucklebones

1 Each player places her playing pieces on the board in
the starting position.

2 The cow may not move at any time during the
game.

3 The player with the calf moves first. He moves the
piece to an open position along the linking line. The
calf cannot jump an occupied position.

4 The player moving the cowboys tries to corner the
calf at the other end of the board.

5 The calf wins if it makes it to the position occupied
by the cow.

DID YOU KNOW?
This game is traditionally played using knucklebones from a sheep. Each side of the knucklebone represents one of the characters.

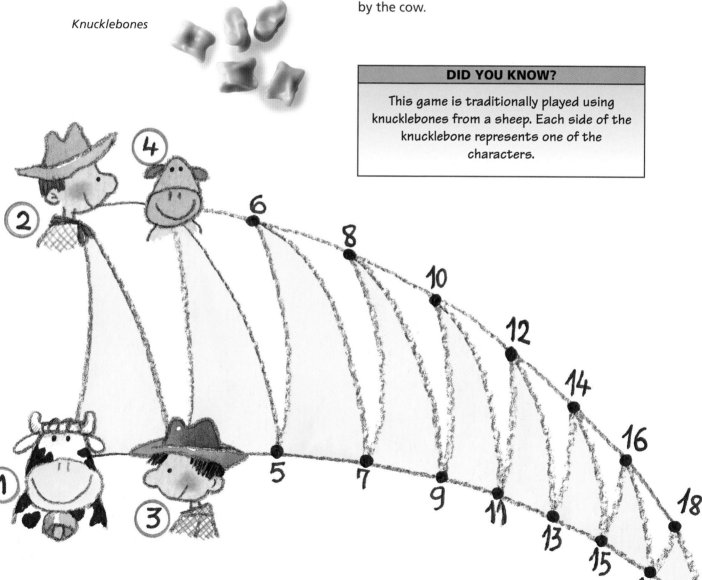

Hopscotch

This is a traditional game played across five continents. A drawing is made on the ground, a flat pebble is tossed inside the diagram, and the players hop inside the drawing.

Some researchers associate this game with practices used by some to predict the future. Presently, this game is played primarily by girls.

There are basically two variations of this game: the hopscotch in which the players hop or jump, and the hopscotch in which the players kick the pebble or quoit into place.

Kicking the Pebbles

1 In all variations of this game, the pebble is tossed into the first box. One of the players hops into the box on one foot and kicks the pebble from box to box using the foot on the ground until she gets to the end.

2 If she makes it, she starts again, tossing the pebble into the second box. The game ends when one of the players is able to move the pebble through each one of the boxes.

3 If the pebbles land on a line or if the player steps on a line, she loses her turn.

The Cookie

Basque region (Spain and France)

In this version, the pebble is kicked from one box into the next using both feet together.

The Cat

Spain

The first toss goes into the lower right-hand box; the second toss goes into the cat's mouth. This procedure is repeated until all the features of the cat have been played.

The cat's nose is a resting area.

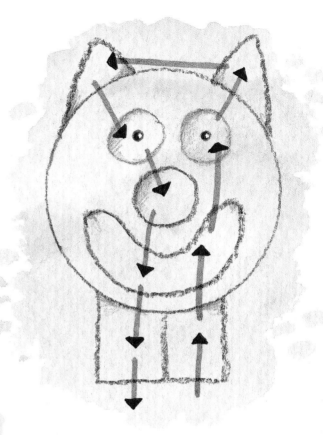

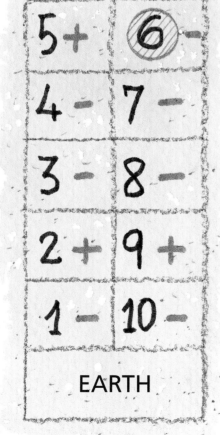

The Moon

Holland

Players must hop with one foot in the squares marked with a – symbol. The squares marked with a + symbol require the player to jump with both feet. Neither the pebble nor the player may land in the moon circle in box 6, but they still must land inside box 6. When the players reach box 10, they should reverse the play until they reach the Earth box.

The Spider

Mallorca, Spain

In this version of the game, neither the pebble nor the player's foot may touch a number or a line.

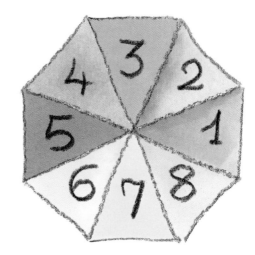

Square Bed

Scotland

If you want to make this game more difficult, alter the order of the numbers; the farther apart they are, the more difficult the game will be.

The Snail

France

This hopscotch game is shaped like a snail and may be found in different parts of the world with different playing rules.

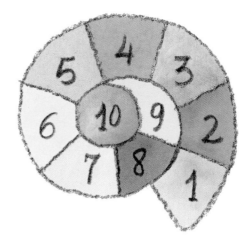

The Quoit

Mexico

The player must remove the pebble from the grid with only one kick. When one of the players gets to the crown, she draws a smaller one inside. (Up to three crowns are suggested.) The winner is the player who kicks the pebble out of the third crown.

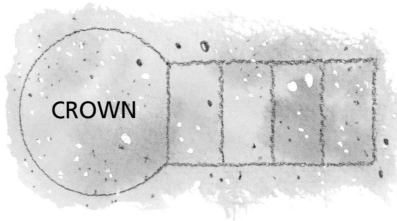

Joz bazi

Afghanistan

1 A player tosses a pebble into the first box, hops inside on one foot, and kicks the pebble out of that square.

2 After the first turn, box 1 may not be entered again.

3 The player then tosses the pebble into the second box, hops inside, and kicks the pebble out.

4 The rest of the game continues the same way. The pebble may be kicked multiple times.

5 If the player's foot or pebble touches a line or if both of the player's feet touch the ground, he loses his turn and the next player starts.

6 When one of the players has jumped through all the boxes successfully, it is time to "travel through the desert" without stepping on any of the lines. The playmates choose how he will get to box 6:
• blindfolded, or
• crawling with both hands and one foot on the ground with the other foot in the air (the foxtail).

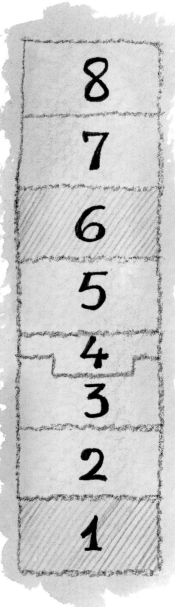

DID YOU KNOW?

In many predominantly Christian countries, players often write the word "heaven" at the end of the drawing.

Hopping

1 The player tosses the pebble into the first box.

2 The player moves around the game diagram by hopping on one leg and jumping over the box that contains the pebble.

3 When the player gets to the last box, she hops back to the box marked number 2. Once there, she picks up the pebble from the first box, jumps over that box and out of the game diagram.

4 Now, she tosses the pebble to the second box and continues playing as before, always picking up the pebble from its box before she jumps out and tosses again.

5 If the pebble lands on a line, or if the player steps on a line or touches the ground with both feet, she loses her turn. When it is her turn again, the player will continue the game, tossing the pebble from where it was.

6 The winner is the first player to cover all the numbered boxes.

Potsie

New York

Players are not allowed to jump inside the box containing the pebble.

Players can land on both feet in the double boxes (1-2, 4-5, and 7-8), except when the pebble is in one of them.

When a player reaches boxes 7 and 8, she has to quickly turn around and go back to the start.

Amarela
Brazil

The version of hopscotch shown here is from Brazil, but it is also played in the Ukraine. Children there call it *Shagui* and call the final circle "sun" instead of "heaven."

Days of the Week
Holland, Spain, and several Latin American countries

In this version, the only resting place on the game diagram is the box labeled Sunday. Players always start with both feet in the box labeled Earth.

Neca
Mozambique

Here is the design for the playing grid for another traditional game of hopscotch found in many parts of the world, including Mozambique.

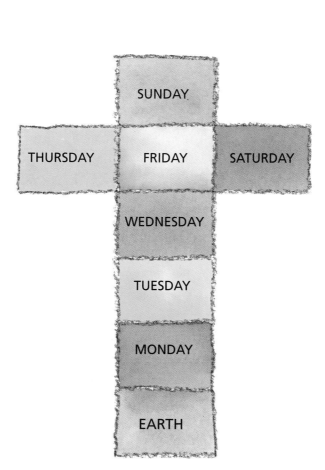

Games with the Balero

The balero is a small toy made from a stick with a tapered end and either a cup with a small mouth or a ball. The cup or ball is tied to the stick with a piece of string.

Chantar

Bolivia

Two basic positions can be used to play with the balero: one traditionally used by boys and one traditionally used by girls.

Boys' Position

1 The player holds the balero by the handle while the ball or cup hangs motionless at the end of the string.

2 He flicks his wrist to move the ball or cup at the end of the string.

3 The object of the balero is to catch the ball/cup on the tapered end of the stick.

Girls' Position

1 The starting position is the same as above, but the player makes the ball/cup swing.

2 The player, again, flicks her wrist to move the ball/cup upward in a curve.

3 The object is the same in both versions: to catch the ball/cup on the tapered end of the stick.

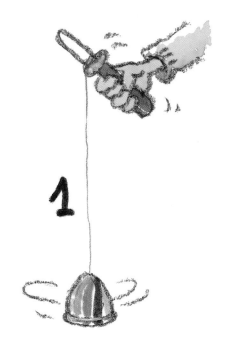

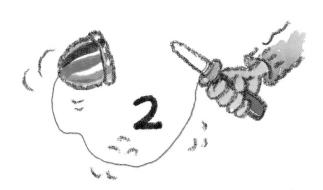

Capirucho

Mexico

1 To start, the tapered end of the handle is inserted in the ball/cup, and the player holds the string with his other hand.

2 He dislodges the ball/cup and tries to insert it again.

Florete

Bolivia

1 The player holds the balero by the handle and lets the ball/cup hang.

2 She twirls the ball/cup from the string, making circles in the air.

3 At the right moment, she jerks the handle and tries to land the ball/cup back onto the tapered end of the balero.

One Hundred

Mexico

1 The players decide their playing order.

2 A player adds points to his or her score according to the figures he or she makes. For example:
- five points for every score with the cup in the boys' position;
- ten points for a capirucho;
- twenty points for every score with the cup in the girls' position.

3 If a player cannot score using any of the figures, he or she passes the balero on to the next player.

4 The next time he or she plays, his or her score is the same as when he or she lost his turn.

5 The winner is the first player to score 100 points.

DID YOU KNOW?

The balero appears in traditional cultures all over America, Asia, and Europe.

Games of Chance

Games of chance are important in many traditional games around the world. Dice with two, four, and six faces have been used for thousands of years to move playing pieces around a game board.

Bul

Played by the Mopan Maya peoples and the k'echi in southern Belize

- **Number of players:** 2 teams with an equal number of players
- **Materials:** 20 small objects to create the playing board. (If there are more than 10 players, the game will need 25 objects. If there are more than 16 players, 30 pieces are needed.) Five playing pieces for each player; 4 two-sided dice.

DID YOU KNOW?
Originally, Bul was played only by men during a thanksgiving ceremony. They played for fun and did not care who was the winner.

Aj Sayil version ("The Ant")

1 Each team sits with their "board" arranged so that their "home" is to their left.

2 Players decide which team goes first. All the players on that team play before the players on the second team do.

3 A player may have only one piece in play at a time.

4 Each player rolls the dice twice and then moves his piece according to the value of the dice.

5 If the value of the dice is (see above):
• 1 marked side: 1 move
• 2 marked sides: 2 moves
• 3 marked sides: 3 moves
• 4 marked sides: 4 moves
• No side marked: 5 moves.

6 Each team begins at home. When a piece gets to the opposing team's home it starts back again. Going into an opponent's home does not require an exact roll of the dice.

7 When a piece falls on an opponent's, the player keeps both pieces, putting one on top of the other, forming a pile of pieces (A). As the player moves around the board, he takes the opponent's piece with his. This pile of pieces may be captured by another single piece or another opponent's pile. There is no limit to the number of piles that can be captured (B).

8 If a piece falls on a piece that belongs to another member of the same team, nothing happens.

9 When the first player arrives home, he must use a new piece on his next turn.

10 When a pile of pieces arrives home, the pieces are distributed among the players. The pieces belonging to the opposite team are captured and do not enter again.

11 The game is over when a team has no pieces left to enter. The winner is the team with the most captured pieces.

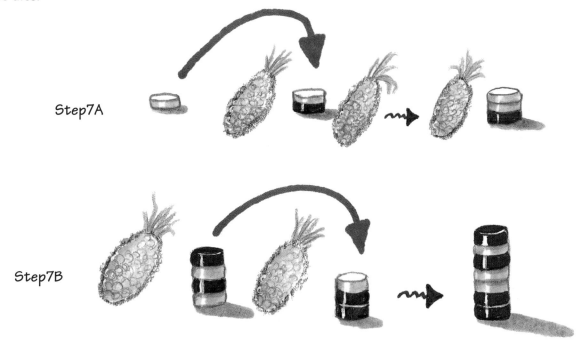

Step7A

Step7B

Mon s'hi mo ut

Played by the Cheyenne Indians

- **Number of players:** 2 to 5
- **Material:** 5 flat stones—all have one unmarked side, 2 stones have a bear print painted on one side, and the other 3 stones have a cross painted on them; a dish or a basket; and 8 small sticks per player

1 Two teams sit facing each other. Each player places the 8 sticks in the middle.

2 Each player takes a turn with the basket, tossing the stones into the air, and catching them again with the basket.

3 According to the combination made by the stones (see below), the player picks up a certain number of sticks.

4 The players who end up with all the opponent's sticks wins the game.

Step3

Winning combinations :

- 5 blank sides: each player on the throwing team picks up a stick
- 3 blank and 2 bear prints: 1 stick
- 1 blank, 2 prints, and 2 crosses: 1 stick
- 2 blank and 3 crosses: 3 sticks
- 2 prints and 3 crosses: 8 sticks and the game

Losing combinations:

- 2 blank sides, 2 prints, and a cross: each member of the team leaves a stick in the middle
- 4 blank and 1 print: lose 1 stick

Ad elta stelpur

("The Maiden Hunt")

Iceland

- **Number of players:** 2
- **Material:** a board, 6 playing pieces per player, and 2 dice

1 Each player takes a turn rolling the dice.

2 Game pieces are moved only if the dice show:
- 2 sixes: 4 pieces advance 6 spaces each
- A six and a different value: 1 piece advances 6 spaces
- A one and a different value: 1 piece advances 1 space.
- Any double (except six): 2 pieces advance as many spaces as the number shown, and the player rolls again

3 Pieces move clockwise.

4 If a piece lands on a space occupied by another piece of the same color, it continues to the next empty space on the board.

5 When a piece lands on a space occupied by an opponent, that piece is captured, removed from the board, and remains out of play.

Step2

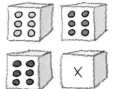

Step3

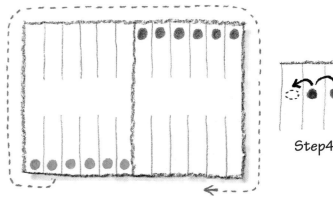

Step4

6 A player's last piece is called the *hornskella* (corner piece). This piece may only be played in the four corners of the board. The *hornskella* moves are illustrated below.

7 The winner is the first player to capture all his opponent's pieces.

Step6

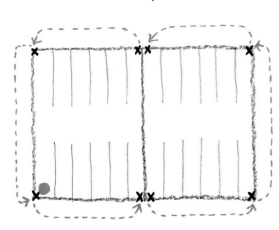

Hornskella moves

- A one:
  advance 1 corner

- A six:
  advance 2 corners

- A double one:
  advance 4 corners

- A double six:
  advance 8 corners

- A double value other than a one or a six: extra turn

To the Finish Line

These games are played on a board, and the different game pieces attempt to reach home before the others. The layout of the boards and how the pieces advance around them make each game unique.

Suag ma

("Horse race")

Laos

• **Number of players:** 4
• **Material:** a board (see page 124) and 4 different pieces; 3 stones per player

1 The player to go first is the one who draws the shortest stick.

2 Each player is assigned three numbers:
• The player with the shortest stick receives 1, 5, and 9.
• The second player gets 2, 6, and 10.
• The third gets 3, 7, and 11.
• The fourth gets 4, 8, and 12.

3 Each player places her piece at one starting point.

4 Each player hides some or all of her stones in her hand (from 0 to 3).

5 When the signal is given, the players show the stones in their hands. The player with the number assigned in step 2 that matches the total number of stones moves first.

6 Players move one space at a time, according to the numbers they have been given.

7 If the space is occupied, she goes back one space.

8 When a player has covered the entire outer square, she starts the second square on her next turn. This second square has to be completely covered before playing the inner square.

9 The winner is the first player to reach the center.

Each player occupies one of the starting points.

3·7·11

4·8·12

2·6·10

1·5·9

The players show 7 stones. The player who has number 7 will begin the game.

Step 8

The Royal Game of Ur

Mesopotamia (modern-day Iraq and Syria)

• **Number of players:** 2
• **Material:** a board with 20 squares, 3 pyramidal dice with 2 painted tips, and 7 playing pieces per player

1 The players decide who starts.

2 All pieces start off the board.

3 Each player takes turns rolling the three dice. The possible moves are
• 3 painted tips: advance 5 squares or introduce a piece onto the board and throw again
• 3 unpainted tips: advance 4 squares and throw again
• 2 unpainted tips: no move and lose a turn
• 1 unpainted tip: advance 1 square and lose a turn

4 To enter a piece on the board, the player must throw 3 painted tips.

5 Each square may only hold 1 piece. If a piece falls on a square occupied by an opponent, the piece is bumped and returned to its owner, who may play it again.

6 An exact roll of the dice is needed to move a piece off the board.

7 The winner is the first player to remove all his pieces.

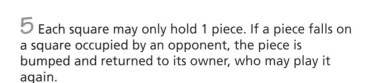

Step 3

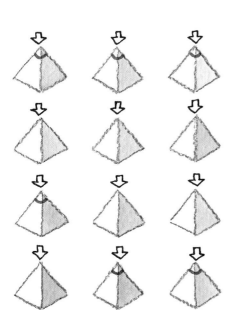

Step 5

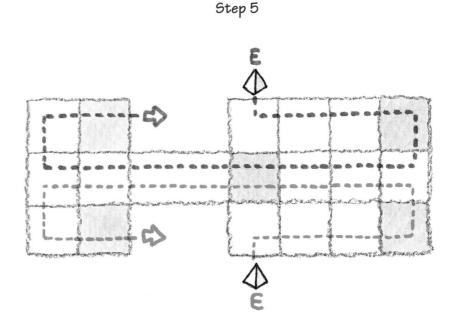

Games with Marbles

Marbles are made out of different hard substances such as cooked clay, glass, or steel. Nature also provides us with small objects that may be used for marble games, including seeds, grains, or dried fruits.

Games to play on plain boards

Kelereng

Indonesia

- **Number of players:** 2 to 6
- **Material:** a piece of chalk or a stick to mark the ground and about 8 marbles per player

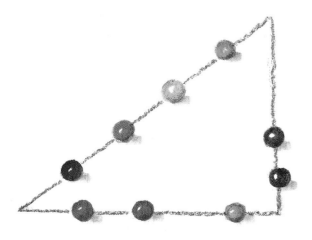

1 Draw a triangle on the ground. Each player places an agreed number of marbles on the lines of the triangle.

2 Each player takes a turn throwing her marble from the throwing line. If she hits any of the marbles in the triangle, she keeps it and throws again from where her original marble landed.

3 If no marble is hit, the player loses her turn.

4 When there are no more marbles left on the lines that form the triangle, then the players will try to hit the opponents' with their own. If one player hits another's marble, the loser gives up that marble, along with all the other marbles he has won up to that time.

5 The winner of the game keeps all the marbles that were used in the game.

Two ways to throw marbles

DID YOU KNOW?

In Catamarca, Argentina, two children may play a game called "Quema" (burn). One child throws a marble a long distance while the other tries to hit ("burn") it. If he fails, the first player will try to hit his friend's. Each time a burn is made, the loser pays an agreed-upon number of marbles.

The Circle

Asturias, Spain

• **Number of players:** 2 to 6
• **Material:** a piece of chalk or a stick to mark the ground; about 8 marbles per player

1 A circle about 10 feet (3 m) wide is drawn on the ground.

2 Each player takes a turn throwing one of his marbles, trying to knock another player's marble out of the circle.

3 Every time a player hits a marble out of the circle, he keeps it.

4 If one marble knocks another out of the circle but remains inside the circle itself, the player gets another turn.

5 If both the hit marble and the thrown marble roll out of the circle, that player loses his turn.

6 If no marbles are knocked out of the circle, the player loses his turn and throws his marble from the same place on his next turn.

7 The game is over when there are no more marbles inside the circle.

Players agree on the number of marbles to place in the circle in the shape of a cross.

A Line of Balls

Cantón Sanandita, Bolivia

- **Number of players:** 2 to 6
- **Material:** a piece of chalk or a stick to mark the ground and about 8 marbles per player

1 Players throw their marbles to see who will go first. The player whose marble comes closest to any one of the lines starts the game.

2 From where the marbles came to a stop, each player throws her marble toward the intersection of the lines. She keeps any of the marbles she hits.

3 The same player continues to toss her marbles until she misses.

4 Once all the marbles on the lines are gone, players try to hit other marbles wherever they are. Any marble that gets hit is kept by the player who hits it.

5 The game is over when there are no more marbles.

The Board

France

- **Number of players:** 2 to 6
- **Material:** several marbles for each player and a flat piece of wood

1 Each player takes turns rolling one of his marbles from the upper end of the board.

2 The player who succeeds in hitting any one marble on the ground keeps them all.

This game is played on a flat surface. Make as many horizontal lines as there are players. Players agree how far the throwing line will be from the horizontal lines.

Marble games on a pitted surface

Jogo dos berlindes

Portugal

- **Number of players:** 2 to 6
- **Material:** 8 marbles per player

1 Make three holes in the ground in a straight line about 20 inches (50 cm) long.

2 In turn, each player tries to land a marble in the first hole.

3 When a player succeeds in landing his marble in all three holes, he can hit the other players' marbles and keep them.

4 When no marbles remain, the game is over.

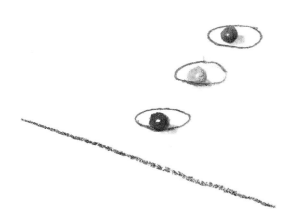

Boliyoyo Capital

Nicaragua and Guatemala

- **Number of players:** 2 to 6
- **Material:** 8 marbles per player

1 Make 4 holes in the ground forming a square (they may be numbered) and a fifth hole in the middle, called "Guatemala."

2 Each player tries to land a marble in the first hole. Each player proceeds to try and land a marble in each of the other holes before her opponents do.

3 Once a marble lands in a hole, the next throw is made from that position.

4 Players may try to hit another player's marbles to interrupt his progress.

5 A marble is eliminated from the game once it has been hit three times.

6 Once a player hits the central hole, she may shoot from that position to try to hit any other marble.

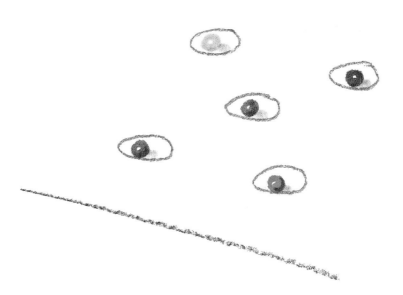

DID YOU KNOW?

In Japan there is a very similar game called tengoku-jigoku ("Heaven and Hell"). Each player starts from heaven, tries to roll his marble into the hole for hell, and then follows the series 2, 1, 2, 3, 2 to go back to heaven. All marbles hit on the way are eliminated.

Hide and Seek

Hide and seek is a game that can be played by 2 players or 2 groups.

Sey

Played by the Dogon Tribe in Mali

- **Number of players:** 2
- **Material:** dirt and a stone

1 Draw a circle on the ground. Both players sit facing each other. Each player makes three holes in the ground.

2 They decide who starts. That player takes a small stone, called a *tibi,* and mixes it with some dirt from the ground. He carefully lets the dirt seep through his closed fist, trying not to let the other player see where he drops the tibi.

3 When the three holes are filled with dirt from the player's hand, the opponent guesses where he thinks the tibi is. If he guesses correctly, he gets the tibi and it is his turn to hide it.

4 If the player successfully hides the tibi without his opponent finding it, he makes another hole to the right of his first three holes and hides the tibi again.

5 The winner is the player whose holes extend to meet his opponent's holes.

6 Every time a new game starts, the holes are emptied out.

Sinko lukai

("The Hidden Stick")

Nepal

• **Number of players:** 2
• **Material:** a small thin stick and some sand

1 Make an elongated mound with the sand, approximately 2 feet (60 cm) long.

2 The player who starts pushes the stick into the side of the mound and takes it out again on the opposite side two or three times. Then she leaves the stick hidden inside the mound without her opponent seeing where.

3 The other player puts his hands together, crosses his fingers, places them where he believes the stick is hidden, and digs into the sand.

4 If he guesses correctly, it is his turn to hide the stick.

5 The best of 5 games wins.

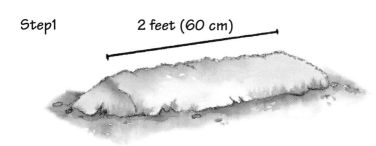

Step1   2 feet (60 cm)

Step2

Flongodo

Played by the Fula people in Ivory Coast, Mali, and Burkina Faso

• **Number of players:** 2
• **Material:** a stick (or stone) for each player to use as a marker and another small stone

1 Each player sets his marker in the first box.

2 One of the players hides the stone in one hand while the other guesses in which hand it is hidden.

3 If he guesses correctly, he keeps the stone and takes his turn hiding it. If he guesses incorrectly, the player who hid the stone advances his marker one box and hides the stone again.

4 The winner is the first player to move his marker to the center.

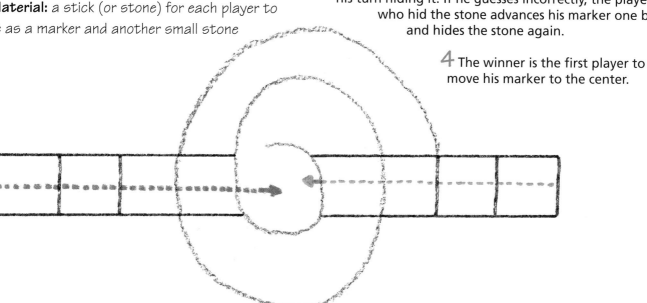

Mukesinnah dahdewoo

("The Moccasin Game")

Played by the Chippewa in North America

- **Number of players:** 2 players or 2 teams
- **Material:** 4 shoes, 4 stones (one with a mark), and 20 sticks

1 Both players sit facing each other. One of the players hides the stones under the shoes (see steps 3 and 4) and the other player tries to find it. (If the game is played by two teams, the whole team looks for the stone.)

2 The 20 sticks are used to count points and are distributed among the players according to the rules detailed in step 5.

3 A player places one of the 4 stones under each shoe.

4 The other player (or team) watches carefully and then guesses which shoe hides the marked stone. If the guess is wrong, he keeps guessing until he finds it.

5 The score depends on how many guesses it takes to find the marked stone.
- If he guesses right on his first try, the player who hid the stone gets 4 sticks.
- If he guesses right on the second try, the player who hid the stone gets only 3 sticks.
- If he guesses right on his third try, then the person guessing gets 3 sticks.
- If he guesses right on his fourth try, the player who hid the stone gets 4 sticks.

6 The game is over when the 20 sticks have been distributed and the winner is the player who has the most sticks.

Obraczka

("The Ring")

Poland

- **Number of players:** more than 6
- **Material:** a ring or a key, and a piece of string or rope long enough to be held by all the players at the same time

1 The string is threaded through the ring and both ends are tied into a knot.

2 A player is chosen to be It. The other players sit forming a circle. It stands in the center of the circle.

3 All the players hold the string with both hands. It turns his back and one player takes hold of the ring. (The player who is It may also be blindfolded.)

4 The players start singing and slide the ring from hand to hand. When the song is over, It turns around and tries to guess who has the ring.

5 It keeps standing in the center of the circle until she guesses who is hiding the ring. When she guesses correctly, the player who was hiding the ring becomes the new It and stands in the center of the circle.

L'anell picapedrell

("The Hidden Ring")

Played in Catalan-speaking areas of Andorra, Spain, France, and Italy

• **Number of players:** 6 to 20
• **Material:** a ring

1 The player who is It takes the ring in her hands while the other players sit around her with their hands cupped together.

2 It drops the ring into the hands of one of the players so that no one else knows who receives it.

3 After she has gone from player to player, It shows she no longer has the ring and asks one of the players, "Do you know who has the ring?"

4 This player says a name. If the player whose name is mentioned does not have it, then it is his turn to say someone's name. The procedure is repeated until the ring is found.

5 The player who discovers the ring will be the next It.

Step 2

Kubb

Although the origin of this game is unknown, documents show that the Vikings played Kubb on the Island of Gotland in the year 1000 A.D. Since 1995, the island has celebrated with an international Kubb tournament.

Kubb

Sweden

- **Number of players:** 2 to 12
- **Material:** a piece of chalk or other material to mark the ground; a 4-by-4-by-12-inch (9-by-9-by-30-cm) wooden box (the king); 10 wooden pieces (the kubbs) about 3 by 3 by 2 inches (7 by 7 by 5 cm); and 6 round sticks (the throwing sticks) about 1¾ inch by 1 foot (44 mm by 30 cm) long.

1 Players form two teams and stand behind the throwing line.

2 Team number 1 distributes the sticks among its members.

3 Every player from team number 1 takes a turn throwing his stick at the kubbs belonging to team number 2.

4 When all members of a team have thrown their sticks, it is the other team's turn.

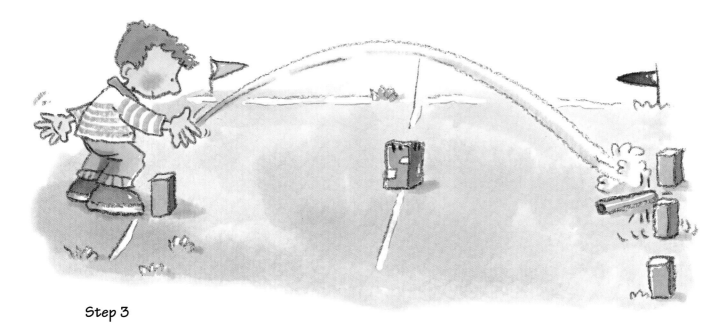

Step 3

5 A kubb is removed from the playground every time an opponent knocks it down. Then team number 2 throws the kubb back into team number 1's field, trying to knock down team number 1's kubbs.

6 If after three attempts a player misses the kubb or throws it out of limits, a player from the other team may place that kubb wherever he wants.

7 When throwing the sticks, the first kubbs that should be knocked down are the ones that sit off-line in the opponents' field. The kubbs on the line that are knocked down don't count until the others have been eliminated.

8 Once a team has knocked down all the opponents' kubbs and moved them into their own field, they can attempt to knock down the king.

9 The king may be knocked down only when all the kubbs are in their own field.

10 The team whose player knocks down the king is the winner.

11 If during play the king is knocked down (whether with a stick or a kubb), that team loses and the game is over.

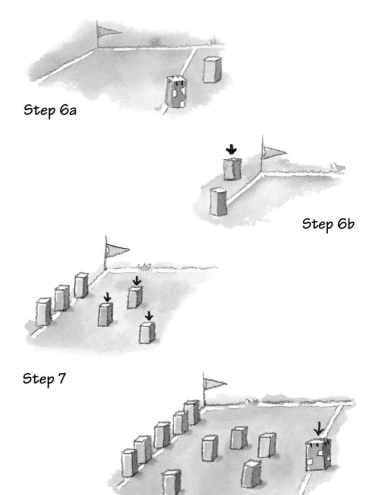

Step 6a

Step 6b

Step 7

Step 8

Two-Team Games

Munhanganing

Played by Australian aborigines in Arnhem Land, northern Australia

- **Number of players:** 2 teams of up to 20 members each
- **Material:** a piece of chalk to mark the ground

1 One team is called the *Munhanganing* (gecko or lizard) and the other is the *Wurrurlurl* (fly).

2 The Munhanganing team disperses itself over the playground, and the Wurrurlurl team starts the game from outside the marked area.

3 When the signal is given, the defenders chase their opponents, trying to tag them.

4 When one of the players on the offense is tagged or steps outside the playing area, she waits in the middle of the field until all the other players on her team are tagged.

5 When all the players have been tagged, the teams switch roles.

The game is played in a large area with a square drawn in the middle. The square must be large enough to hold all the members of a team.

Gallova

Aragon, Spain

• **Number of players:** *20 to 30*

1 Two teams are formed: offense (A) and defense (B).

2 One player from the A team is It while his teammates form a circle around him.

3 The players from the B team disperse over the playground.

4 When the game begins, the B players try to hop on the back of the A players.

5 If It tags one of the players on the B team, that player becomes a prisoner and must stay inside the circle. If anyone on the B team crosses into the circle without being tagged, all his playmates are freed.

6 If the player who crosses into the circle is tagged before getting out, he and all the other players remain inside the circle.

7 If one of the players on team B is on the back of one of the A team players and falls off, his teammates are freed and the game continues.

8 The player who is It should wait until one of the players on horseback falls off before tagging him. When this happens, the game ends and the teams switch roles.

9 The game ends when all the players on team B are on the backs of the players forming the circle.

Kabaddi

Played in India, Bangladesh, Pakistan,
Sri Lanka, Thailand, Nepal, Japan, and Malaysia.

• **Number of players:** 2 teams of 8 members each

1 Two teams are formed. The defending team is on the playing field and the offensive team is off the field.

2 One member of the offense runs onto the playing field and tries to tag as many members of the opposite team as possible.

3 This player must yell *"Kabaddi!"* until he is out of breath.

4 If the player takes a breath while on the field, he is out of the game and the roles are reversed: the offense becomes the defense and vice versa.

5 If the player leaves the field without taking a breath, all the tagged members of the defending team are out of the game.

6 If the player is tagged by a defender before crossing the line, he is out of the game. The teams switch roles.

7 When the teams switch roles, the members of the defending team who were eliminated by being tagged may not go back into the game.

8 When players from the defense are eliminated along with players from the offense, players may return to the game in the same number as the eliminated players of the opposite team.

9 The game is over when one of the teams has lost all its players.

As many players go onto the playing field as there are eliminated players from one team.

Jo jo

Played in Bangladesh and India

• **Number of players:** between 10 and 20, divided into 2 teams

1 A rectangular playing field is divided into two equal parts.

2 Two teams are formed:
• The defense: all members except one sit along the dividing line of the playing field.
• The offense: all members stay outside the playing field.

3 A player from each team is chosen to be It.

4 When the signal is given, the player who is It for the offense steps onto the playing field, where he will be able to move around freely.

5 The player who is It for the defense tries to tag her opponent.

6 If the player for the offense crosses the dividing line, the defender may not cross the line to tag him. She pats the back of one of the players sitting along the dividing line and yells "jo jo." That player becomes the new defender and can only move in her half of the playing field.

7 When the defending player tags the chased player, the latter leaves the playing field and a new player from the offense steps in.

8 The game is over when all the members of the offense team have been tagged.

DID YOU KNOW?

In some towns this game is played only by girls.

Efdáriz

Played by the Bereber people of Northern Africa

• **Number of players:** between 10 and 20, divided into 2 teams

1 All the players take their positions on opposite sides of the field, where they are safe.

2 When a player goes onto the playing field, he may be tagged by an opposing team member who entered the playing field after he did.

3 When a player is tagged, he is taken to the opposite team's area. While a player is taking an opponent to her own area, she may not be tagged by an opponent.

4 The tagged player is saved when a player from his own team tags him.

5 The game is over when all the players of a team have been captured.

Hand Games

Played everywhere in the world by two or more people.

Jan ken pon

("Rock, Paper, Scissors")

Japan

• **Number of players:** 2

1 Players stand facing each other.

2 At the signal, each player shows her hand in one of the following positions:
• Rock: a closed fist
• Paper: palm down flat
• Scissors: forefinger and middle finger extended forward

3 The winner is based on the following:
• The rock can crush a scissors (the rock wins)
• Scissors can cut paper (the scissors wins)
• Paper can be wrapped around the rock (paper wins)

4 The best of five games wins.

DID YOU KNOW?

The origin of Jan ken pon is uncertain, although it may have started in China. Zyanken is a Japanese word of Chinese origin meaning "two fists," and pon is probably a nonsense word.

Rock

Paper

Scissors

Wan, tu, zum

Malaysia

• **Number of players:** 2

1 Players stand facing each other, their hands hidden behind their backs.

2 The game starts with both players saying "*wan, tu, zum*," and as they say "*zum*," they show one hand, making one of the following signs:
• A bird: the tips of the five fingers closely touching each other
• A rock: a closed fist
• A pistol: forefinger and thumb extended in imitation of a gun
• A table: an open hand palm down
• Water: an open hand palm up

3 The winner is decided according to the following:
• The bird drinks water
• The rock hits the bird
• The pistol breaks the rock
• The pistol breaks the table
• The pistol kills the bird
• Water drowns the rock
• Water drowns the pistol
• The table floats in water
• The table hurts the bird

4 If both players show the same sign, the game is repeated.

5 The number of games to play should be decided before the players begin.

Bird   Rock   Pistol   Table   Water

Machha machha bhyaguto

("The Fish and the Frog")

Nepal

• **Number of players:** 2

1 Players sit facing each other. One is the fisherman and the other is both a fish (*machha*) and a frog (*bhyaguto*).

2 The fish is represented by an extended forefinger and the frog by the thumb.

3 The challenged player forms the fish and moves his forefinger rapidly in front of the fisherman while repeating "*Machha, machha . . .*"

4 The fisherman tries to catch the fish, and the fish tries to avoid being caught by quickly replacing the finger with the thumb (the frog).

5 When the fish is caught, the players switch roles.

Hipitoi

Played by the Maori people of New Zealand

• **Number of players:** 2

1 Players stand facing each other. During each turn, one player begins and the other responds.

2 Each player makes any of the following fist formations:
• Two closed fists
• Two thumbs up
• Right thumb up
• Left thumb up

3 One player starts by saying "*hipitoi,*" and the other responds with "*ra.*"

4 The first player says "*hipitoi*" again and makes one of the four possible hand signs, while the other player also makes one.

5 If both hand signs are different, the player who started gets 0 points but says "*hipitoi*" again and makes another hand sign.

6 If both signed the same, the player that says "*hipitoi ra,*" before the other player makes another sign, wins the round.

7 The player who yells "*hipitoi ra*" as described above starts the new round.

8 The player who began the game can win by being very quick with his movements.

9 The best of 10 rounds wins.

Morra

Played in the Mediterranean areas of Spain and Italy

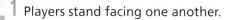

• **Number of players:** 2

1 Players stand facing one another.

2 At a signal, both players show the fingers of one hand at the same time, and they guess how much they think the fingers will add up to (maximum is 10).

3 If they guess wrong, they repeat the procedure until one of the players gets the correct answer.

4 When one of the players guesses correctly, she says *"mia"* and gets a point.

5 If one of the players guesses correctly, but it goes unnoticed, she misses the point.

6 The game ends when one of the players makes the number of guesses agreed upon at the beginning of the game (usually 21).

Gachanko

Japan

• **Number of players:** 2 teams of 3 to 8 players each
• **Material:** a piece of chalk to mark the ground

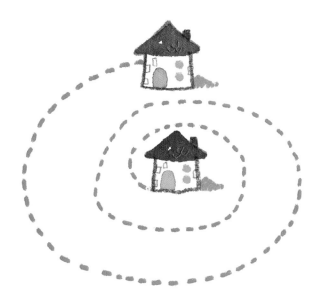

1 Draw a spiral on the ground. The ends of the spiral are home to each team.

2 The teams start at their home bases.

3 When the signal is given, one player from each team begins running inside the spiral.

4 When the players meet, they say *"gachanko"* and start playing *jan ken pon*.

5 The player who loses this round exits the spiral and a new player from his team enters.

6 The winner keeps running in the same direction as before.

7 When these two players meet, they repeat the procedure as explained in step #4.

8 The team with the most players arriving at the opponent's home wins.

Games with Tops

Many objects found in nature can be used as tops, which is a reason why tops are found among cultures in countries as far from each other as China, Egypt, the Amazon, and Papua New Guinea.

Turbo

Played by the ancient Romans

1 A circle is drawn on the ground and divided into 10 uneven sections.

2 Each section gets a number; 1 goes to the largest section and 10 to the smallest.

3 Each player spins his top and receives the points indicated in that section where it lands.

4 Play continues until the points decided at the beginning of the game are reached.

Gasing

Malaysia

• **Number of players:** 2 to 6
• **Material:** a top for each player and a piece of chalk or a stick to draw on the ground

1 A wide circle is drawn on the ground.

2 Each player spins a top inside the circle.

3 The tops will touch one another and some of them will stop spinning.

4 The winner is the last top to stop spinning.

La dura

("The Longest Spin")
Catamarca, Argentina

Number of players: 2 to 6
Material: a top for each player

1 All players spin their tops at the same time.

2 The winner is the player whose top spins the longest.

DID YOU KNOW?

This game is commonly used to decide the order of play in a different game. Sometimes players have to pick the top off the ground to continue the spin in the palm of their hand.

The Round Street

Antioquía, Colombia

1 A circle is drawn on the ground, and one of the players is chosen to leave his top inside the circle.

2 The other players take turns spinning their tops and trying to hit the stationary top out of the circle.

3 If a top does not touch the stationary top, it remains in the circle until someone hits it out.

Ball Games

Ball games have been a part of history for thousands of years. They have been played in ancient Egypt, Mesopotamia, and in the Aztec regions of Mexico.

Box Ball

New York, United States

- **Number of players:** 2 or 4
- **Material:** a piece of chalk and a ball

1 Two squares a little over 1 foot by 1 foot (1 meter by 1 meter) are drawn on the ground.

2 Each one of the players stands in one of the squares, facing his opponent.

3 They decide who starts. That player bounces the ball on the ground, hitting it with his hand and sending it into the opponent's square.

4 Once the ball bounces on the ground, the opponent hits the ball, sending it back to his opponent's square.

5 The game goes on until:
- The ball misses the opponent's square;
- A player misses the ball;
- The ball bounces more than once in a square.

6 The server gets a point every time his opponent misses a hit. If the server misses, the serve goes to the other team.

7 Eleven points wins a match, although the game may also go to 21.

8 The winning score must always be at least 2 points more than the losing team's score.

Cheia

Mozambique

- **Number of players:** 2 teams of 6 players each
- **Material:** a ball, a stick to mark the ground, and a piece of chalk or a bottle

1 The playing field is defined by two parallel lines about 33 feet (10 meters) apart.

2 Create a sand mound in the middle of the field and place a bottle on top.

3 Players choose which team plays offense and which plays defense. One of the players from the defending team stands next to the sand mound.

4 The offensive players stand behind both lines.

5 The defender tries to fill the bottle with sand.

6 The offensive team tosses the ball from one to another, and on the third pass they try to hit the defender.

7 If the defender fills the bottle with sand without being hit by the ball, she empties it while counting up to 100.

8 If the defender catches the ball without dropping it, she can throw it out as far as possible, earning herself time to fill up the bottle up again.

9 When the defender is hit, she leaves the playing field and one of her teammates takes her place on the mound.

10 When all the defenders have been hit by the ball, the roles are switched.

11 The team with the most points wins.

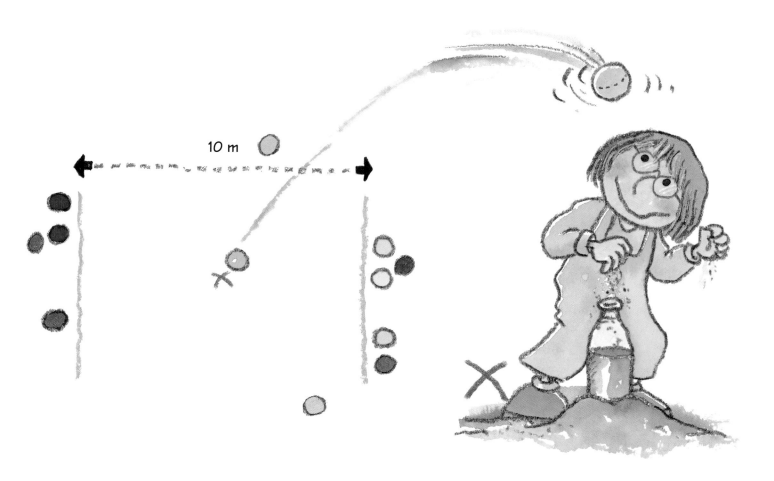

10 m

All in a Row

Games in which pieces are placed in rows have been around for over 4,000 years. These games are played in all parts of the world.

Dara

Gulf of Guinea

- **Number of players:** 2
- **Material:** 12 playing pieces per player and a board with 5 rows of 6 pits each (usually dug in the ground)

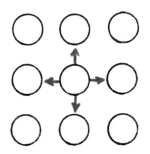

A piece may be moved either horizontally or vertically toward an unoccupied, adjacent position.

1 The game begins with an empty board.

2 Each player takes turns placing one of his pieces in an empty pit.

3 Once all the pieces are placed in the pits, each player moves one piece either horizontally or vertically to an unoccupied adjacent position.

4 When a player succeeds in placing 3 pieces in a row, he takes one of his opponent's pieces off the board.

5 If there are more than 3 pieces in a row the opponent's piece is not removed.

6 A player wins when his opponent has only 2 pieces left.

Sigoga de Tusco

Played by the Nubian people in Sudan and Egypt

Step 1

- **Number of players:** 2
- **Material:** a board divided into 9 squares and 3 playing pieces per player

1 The pieces are lined up in a horizontal row.

2 Each player chooses a different kind of playing piece.

3 Each player takes turns moving one piece to an unoccupied square (it does not have to be an adjacent square).

4 A player wins when he puts 3 pieces in a row, in different positions than their original locations.

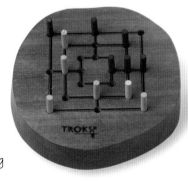

Pieces may be moved toward any empty square.

Molino de doce

Found in an Egyptian temple (1400 B.C.) Very popular in medieval Europe. Versions of this game exist all over the world.

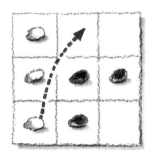

- **Number of players:** 2
- **Material:** a pitted board and 12 playing pieces per player

1 The game starts with an empty board.

2 Each player takes turns placing one piece into an empty pit.

3 When all the pieces are set, the players move them to an unoccupied adjacent position linked by a line. Every time a player gets three of her own pieces in a row, she removes one of her opponent's pieces.

4 A player wins when her opponent has only 2 pieces left.

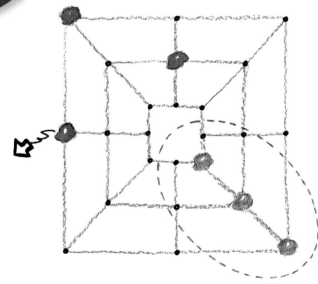

Over the Line

Lines can be drawn on the ground, even when it is covered by snow, using different objects such as a piece of chalk or a stick. Lines are used to mark a playing field, but drawing them may be a game in itself.

Buwan, buwan

("Moon, Moon")

Philippines

- **Number of players:** 3 to 12
- **Material:** Something with which to mark the ground

1 A circle divided into 4 even sections is drawn on the ground. The circle should be large enough so that all the players can run inside it.

2 The player who is It stands in the middle of the circle with his feet on one of the lines.

3 The other players step inside the circle.

4 When the game starts, It begins running on the lines trying to tag one of the players. He can go anywhere as long as he keeps at least one foot on a line.

5 When It tags one of the players inside the circle, that player becomes It in the next game.

Patintero

Philippines, Nepal, Bangladesh, and Mozambique

• **Number of players:** 2 teams with 6 to 10 players each
• **Material:** a piece of chalk or a stick to make lines on the ground

A playing field is drawn with as many lines as there are players. One of the lines must be drawn vertically.

1 Two teams are formed. The players on the team playing offense stand at one end of the playing field.

2 The other team plays defense, and those players each stand on one of the inside lines.

3 When a signal is made, the offensive players enter the playing field. They may not yet be tagged by the defensive team.

4 The members of the defending team may only move along their own lines.

5 When an offensive player tags one of the defenders, the teams switch roles and the game starts again.

6 A team wins when one of its members is able to cross back and forth on the playing field.

Fox and Geese

United States

• **Number of players:** 6 to 12
• **Material:** a piece of chalk or any other object to mark the ground

1 A player is chosen to be It (the fox) and stands in the middle of the circle.

2 The other players occupy any place on a line.

3 When the fox gives the signal, the players start running around on the lines.

4 The game is over when the fox tags a player or when a player runs outside the lines. The person tagged becomes the new fox in the next game.

DID YOU KNOW?

The game Fox and Geese is known by other names as well: Piccadilly, Cut the Pie (in Minnesota), and Wheel Tag. It is played on grass or snow.

Chrome Cards, Matchboxes, Cartetas

In this section you will find games that use small, everyday objects with common features. They are flat and light with a blank side and a marked side.

In the section called "A Game Box" (page 9) you will find easy instructions to make a carteta.

Little Faces

Argentina

- **Number of players:** 2 to 6
- **Material:** 10 cartetas for each player

1 A horizontal line is drawn on a wall. (The height should be agreed on by all the players.)

2 Each player drops a carteta next to the wall.

3 Each player takes a turn dropping a carteta from the height of the line on the wall onto the floor.

4 When a player's carteta falls on one that is already on the floor, he wins all the cartetas dropped until then.

In Medellín, Colombia, the game is played dropping the cartetas from the steps in a staircase.

La Tanguilla

Canary Islands, Spain

- **Number of players:** 2 to 6
- **Material:** a wooden cube (the tanguilla), a shoe heel, a piece of chalk, and at least 5 cartetas per player

1 The tanguilla is placed on the ground. The throwing line is marked a few feet away.

2 Each player stacks one of his cartetas on the tanguilla.

3 Each player takes a turn tossing his heel, trying to knock the cartetas off the tanguilla.

4 The player who knocks the carteta off the tanguilla keeps all the cartetas that are closer to the heel than to the tanguilla.

5 The game is over when there are no more cartetas to play for.

Step 3

Step 4

The Pinch

Catalan-speaking regions

- **Number of players:** 2 to 4
- **Material:** at least 5 cartetas per player

1 Players agree how many cartetas each player will bet.

2 Players place their carteta bets in a pile, face down.

3 Each player takes a turn and hits the pile with one of her cartetas.

4 If some of the cartetas flip over, the player gets to keep the cartetas that fall face up.

5 The game is over when there are no more cartetas in the pile.

Fléndit

Catalan-speaking regions of Spain as well as France, Italy, and Andorra

• **Number of players:** 2 to 6
• **Material:** 5 cartetas for each player and a flat stone

1 A circle is drawn on the ground. The throwing line is marked a few steps away.

2 Each player puts a given number of cartetas inside the circle.

3 Each player takes a turn throwing his flat stone, trying to hit the cartetas. He keeps all the cartetas that are knocked out of the ring.

4 The game is over when there are no cartetas left inside the ring.

The Little Mirror

Argentina

• **Number of players:** 2 to 6
• **Material:** 5 cartetas for each player

1 All players take turns tossing their cartetas against the wall.

2 The player whose carteta falls closest to the wall keeps all the other cartetas tossed by the other players.

3 If the carteta falls and leans against the wall, it is called "the little mirror."

4 Any player who knocks down the little mirror gets to keep all the cartetas.

The Casserole

Aragon, Spain

• **Number of players:** 2 to 6
• **Material:** 5 cartetas for each player, a shoe heel, and an empty can

1 A circle is drawn on the ground and the can set, with the mouth up, in the middle.

2 Each player puts a carteta inside the can.

3 Each player takes a turn throwing the heel from a throwing line.

4 When a player knocks the can over, she keeps all the cartetas that fall outside the ring. The other players put a new carteta inside the can.

5 The game is over when there are no more cartetas left inside the can.

Palmo

Villa Café, Medellín, Colombia

• **Number of players:** 2 to 6
• **Material:** 5 cartetas for each player

1 Each player leaves a carteta on the ground close to a wall.

2 Each player takes a turn throwing his cartetas against the wall, trying to make them bounce off.

3 Cartetas are won by scoring a:
• Pipo (one carteta falls on top of another one); or a
• Cuarta (2 cartetas on the ground are separated by the distance between the thumb and the little finger).

Pipo

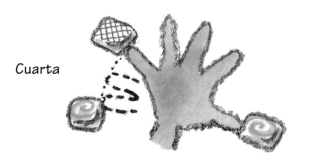
Cuarta

Jumping Games

Jumping, like running, is common practice in children's games and, for this reason, jumping games are found on every continent.

The Jumping Dove

Extremadura, Spain

• **Number of players:** 4 to 20

1 Players divide themselves into groups of two.

2 One pair of players sits on the ground facing each other, their feet touching. The rest of the players stand in a line holding hands with their partners.

3 The first pair of standing players must jump, while holding hands, over the seated couple. But, the seated couple changes positions, becoming increasingly more difficult:
• Legs together
• Open legs
• One foot on top of the other
• The same position but touching one hand
• The same position but touching both hands

4 When all the couples have jumped over the seated couple in each position, the order is repeated, but now the players jump with their feet bound together.

5 If a couple touches the players sitting down while they are jumping over them, they switch roles and the game begins again.

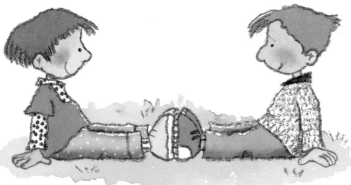

Legs together

Open legs

DID YOU KNOW?

This game is played all over the world in various forms; this version is usually played by girls.

One foot on top of the other

One hand touching

Both hands touching

Hpan hkon dun

("The High Jump")

Burma

This game is played the same way as the Jumping Dove, but the second position (open legs) is excluded. Instead, a fifth hand is added to increase the height that must be jumped, as seen in the illustration to the right.

Jam huay

("Tigers That Cross Lakes")

Thailand

• **Number of players:** 2 to 10

1 A player is chosen to be the lake. The others are the tigers.

2 The player who represents the lake sits on the ground in the first position. The other players jump over her.

3 If a tiger touches the lake when jumping, he becomes the lake, and the game starts again.

4 The game is over when all the tigers have correctly jumped over the five different lake positions shown in the illustration.

First position: dark lake

Second position: deep lake

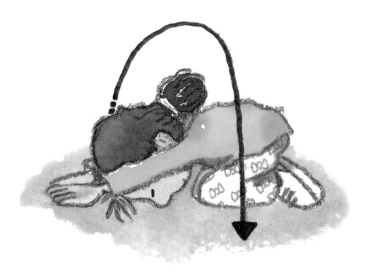

Third position: lake with stones

Fourth position: wide lake

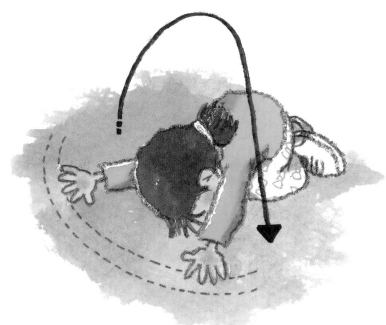

Fifth position: very wide lake

Maklot

Israel

- **Number of players:** 2 to 10
- **Material:** 3 wooden sticks

1 Three sticks are placed on the ground about 1½ feet (half a meter) apart.

2 The players stand in a line.

3 The players take turns jumping over the sticks, with both feet together, without touching the sticks.

4 If a player jumps more than three times over the sticks, touches one of the sticks, or separates his feet, he is out of the game.

5 After all the players have jumped successfully once, the sticks are set farther apart.

6 The winner is the last player left.

DID YOU KNOW?
Pieces of rope or marks made on the ground with a piece of chalk or a stick may also be used in this game.

Five Stone Games

Around the world, small stones or even bones from animals' feet are often used for games. In some places they are games just for boys and in other places they are played by both boys and girls.

Knucklebones

Do tse

("Stone Play")

Tibet

- **Number of players:** 2 to 6
- **Material:** 5 small knucklebones or small stones

1 All the knucklebones are set on the ground.

2 A player picks up a bone from the ground and tosses it into the air. While the bone is in the air, the player picks up another bone from the ground before catching the other.

3 The game goes on until all the bones on the ground have been picked up.

4 At the beginning of the next round, two bones are picked up at a time.

5 In the third round, the player picks up three bones at a time (his opponent decides which three).

6 In the fourth round, the player picks up four bones at a time, tosses them into the air, and catches them with the back of his hand. If any of the bones fall to the ground, they must be picked up before tossing them again. Then they are caught in the palm of the hand again.

7 If a player doesn't pick up the bones from the ground or can't catch the bone in the air, he loses his turn. When it is that player's turn again, he starts from where he left off.

DID YOU KNOW?
In ancient Greece, knucklebones were used to tell the future.

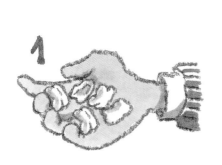

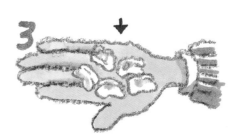

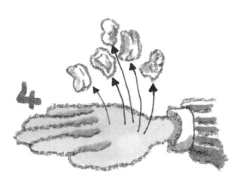

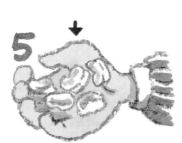

The illustration shows the sequence of movements for the fourth round (Step 6).

La Pallana

Latin America

1 One player tosses all the stones into the air and catches one on the back of her hand. If more than one stone falls on the back of the hand, the player spreads her fingers to let the others drop so only one is left.

2 If all the stones fall off her hand, the player loses her turn.

3 The stone on the back of the hand is tossed into the air again and caught in the palm of the hand.

4 The game starts again and is played the same as Do tse.

DID YOU KNOW?

In Anglo-Saxon countries, people usually play these games using jacks (small, 6-pointed metal objects) and a tiny ball.

Hangman

Catalan-speaking regions of Andorra, France, Spain, and Italy

• **Number of players:** 3 to 8
• **Material:** a knucklebone

1 All the players sit in a circle.

2 Each player takes a turn and tosses the knucklebone on the ground and is assigned the figure represented by the position of the bone.

3 When the bone falls in a position already held by another player, the first player loses that position.

4 When a player has each one of the four figures, he pays a fine.
• The King decides what the fine will be.
• The Grave pays the agreed-upon fine.
• The Hangman makes sure the fine is paid.
• The Guts are free from paying any fine.

King

Grave

Hangman

Guts

The Little Bridge

Chile

1 The player forms a bridge with the forefinger and thumb of one hand.

2 She tosses a stone into the air and, before catching it, tosses one of the other four stones under the bridge.

3 In a variation of this game, the opponent chooses which stone is the last to go under the bridge. In other versions, when all the stones have passed through the bridge, the hand that forms the bridge is lowered to the ground but it must not touch any stone.

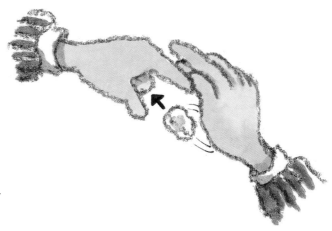

Baby Bones

France

• **Number of players:** 2 to 8
• **Material:** 5 knucklebones, one of them painted a different color

1 The five bones are tossed into the air and caught on the back of the hand.

2 They are tossed into the air again, but this time they are caught in the palm of the hand.

3 The players get one point for each of the bones they catch and two points for the painted bone.

4 All bones held in the palm of the hand are tossed into the air. The game goes on until the five bones drop to the ground.

5 The winner is the player who earns the most points.

Mancala

More than 300 versions of Mancala are found around the world.

Some common features of this game:
- It is played using a pitted board or the ground. Each player has a series of pits.
- Both players use the same seeds.
- Players do not make moves, they *sow*. In order to sow, the seeds are dropped one by one into the pits.

Aualé

West Africa and the Antilles

- **Number of players:** 2
- **Material:** a board with 2 rows of 6 pits and 48 small stones or seeds

1 Players use the row closest to them. To begin, players put four seeds in each pit.

2 Taking turns and moving counterclockwise, a player takes all four seeds out of one of his pits and sows one in each of the next four pits.

Semillas

Step 1

Step 2

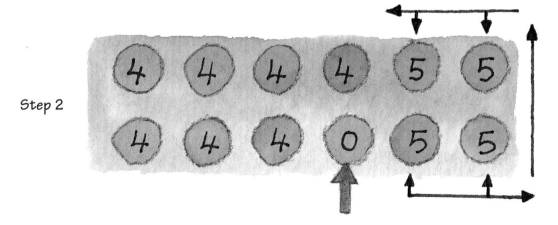

The player takes the four seeds out of the indicated pit and sows them one by one in the corresponding pits as shown in the illustration.

3 If a player makes it all the way around the whole board and still has seeds left, he continues sowing but leaves the initial pit (from which he took the seeds) empty and continues sowing in the next pit.

4 If the second-to-last or the last seed that is sown goes into a pit belonging to the opponent, and if it already has seeds in it, those pits are emptied and the seeds are removed from the board.

However, the seeds cannot be removed without considering two additional rules.

Step 3

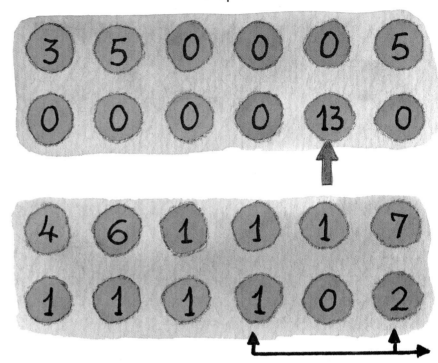

The player starts sowing in the pit marked with an arrow. When there are enough seeds to go around the board and keep sowing, the initial pit remains empty.

Step 4

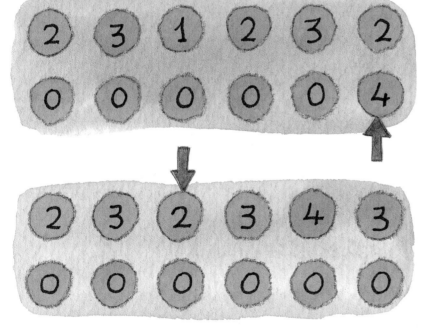

The four seeds in the pit marked with an arrow are removed. Each seed is sown in the next four pits. The last seed falls into the marked pit.

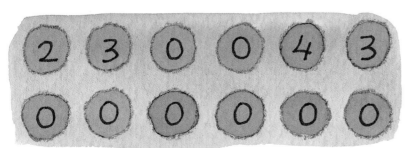

When the play is in the opposite field and there are two or three seeds left in the last two pits just filled, these seeds are captured.

5 The opponent may not be left entirely without seeds. No moves are allowed that would pick up all the opponent's seeds.

6 If all the opponent's pits are empty, the opponent is obliged to sow seeds in the other player's pits.

7 When a player cannot supply seeds to his opponent because he has none left or because the same moves will be repeated, each player gets to keep the seeds he finds in his field.

8 The winner is the player with the highest number of seeds at the end of the game.

DID YOU KNOW?

It is believed that Mancala originated in High Egypt. Now, this game is found all over Africa, the Middle East, and some areas of Asia and Indonesia. The slave trade also brought these games to North America.

Step 5

If the player started sowing seeds after the space marked by an arrow, his seeds would all be captured.

Step 6

You must start sowing from the pit marked by an arrow; this provides the other player with seeds.

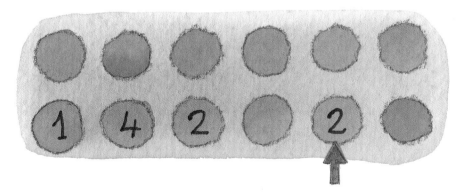

Eson Xorgol

Played by the Kazakh people in northeastern Mongolia

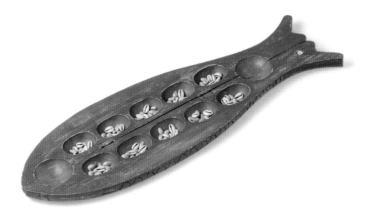

- **Number of players:** 2
- **Material:** a board with 2 rows of 5 pits and 90 seeds

1 The game begins by putting 9 seeds in each of the pits. In this version, the playing field belongs to both players. A player picks all the seeds out of a pit and sows them clockwise one by one.

2 If the sowing ends in a pit with seeds and the one next to it is empty, the player gets to keep all the seeds from the pit next to the empty one.

3 The game is over when there are no more seeds to take.

Step 1

Step 2

DID YOU KNOW?

The Kazakh people usually play this game with goat droppings instead of stones or seeds.

Ba-awa

Played by the Twi people in Ghana. The Yoruba people of Nigeria and Benin call this game "jerin-jerin"

- **Number of players:** 2
- **Material:** *a board with 2 rows of 6 pits and 48 seeds*

1 The game starts with 4 seeds in each pit. In the first round each player starts from the row closest to him.

2 A player takes all the seeds in one of his pits and, sowing counterclockwise, drops them one by one in the pits.

3 If the sowing ends in a pit where there are other seeds, the player takes all the seeds and keeps sowing until the last seed goes into an empty pit.

4 If at any time in the sowing there are 4 seeds in a pit in either field, the owner of the pit removes them.

5 When there are only 8 seeds left on the board, the player who started the game keeps them.

6 When the first round is over, all the seeds go back into the pits. Now each player's field is formed by as many pits as he can fill with the seeds captured during the previous round.

7 The game is over when one of the players controls all 16 pits.

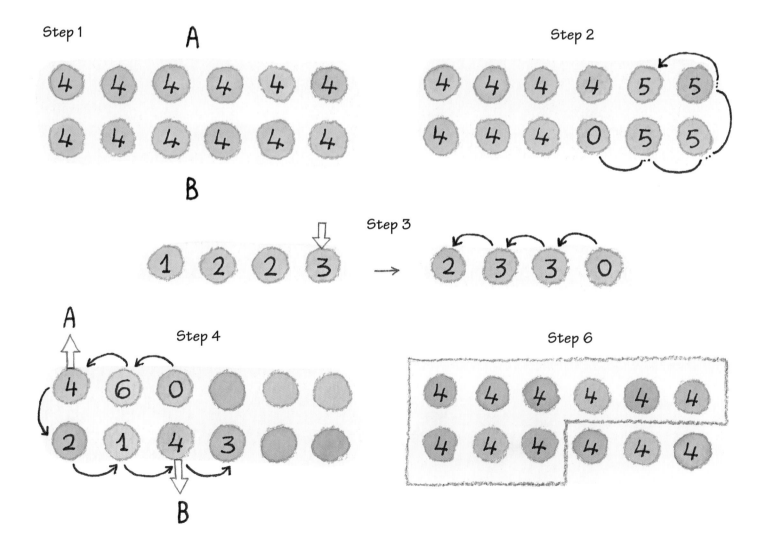

Go

The rules of this game are simple; however, learning to play it well requires lots of study and practice. It is played with white and black stones.

This is a very popular board game in Asian countries. The Japanese call this game Go and made it popular in the western world. In China it is called *Wei-qi* (meaning "board game of enclosure") and in Korea it is called *Baduk*. Now Go players can be found throughout the world.

Go

• Number of players: 2 or 2 teams
• Material: a checker board with 19 horizontal lines and 19 vertical lines and about 60 pieces for each player

1 The game begins with an empty board.

2 The player moving the black stones starts. Moves are made by placing a stone at the intersection of two lines.

3 Once a stone is played it may not be moved again.

4 When a stone, or a group of stones, is surrounded by the opponent's stones, it is captured and removed from the board.

5 If a stone, or group of stones, is placed on the board where it is surrounded by the opponent's stones, it is immediately eliminated.

6 If, when a stone is played, stones in both colors are surrounded, the last player to play her stone is the one who will capture.

7 The game ends when one of the players cannot place any more stones on the board without being captured.

8 The score is determined by counting the stones belonging to each player and the intersections enclosed by each player's stones. The winner is the player who has taken more spaces.

DID YOU KNOW?
Legend says this game was invented in China around the year 2000 B.C., when Emperor Yao Shun asked his advisor to invent a game to develop his son's mental abilities. Apparently, the game was introduced in the Japanese court around 500 A.D. In the 16th century, the game was compulsory in Japanese military schools.

Step 4a

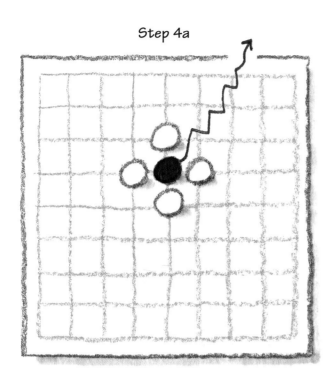

Step 4b

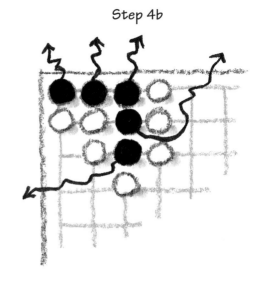

The black stone is surrounded by white stones. Therefore, it is captured and removed from the board.

The white stones surround and capture the black stones.

Step 5

If a white stone were placed in at A, it would be captured immediately.

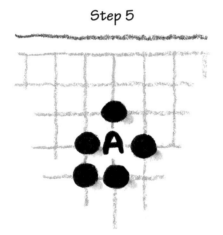

Step 6

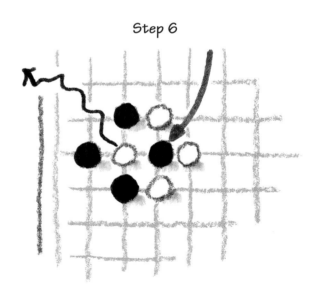

Step 7

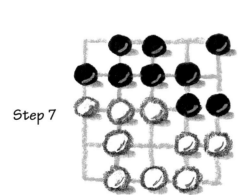

In this illustration using a smaller board, neither player is able to play another stone without being captured. The intersections held by each color are counted; black wins 13 to 12.

Aim and Shoot

An object such as a stone, a shoe heel, or a ball is used to throw at and knock down another object, or aimed at a specified spot.

Ulu maika

Hawaiian Islands

- **Number of players:** between 6 and 12 divided into 2 teams.
- **Material:** a ball and 2 wooden sticks

1 Both sticks are placed on the ground standing up. The starting line is marked a few feet away.

2 Before starting, the players agree on the number of points needed to win the game.

3 The players form two teams and stand behind the starting line.

4 Each player takes a turn trying to roll the ball between the sticks without touching them. If he succeeds, his team gets a point.

5 The team that reaches the agreed-upon number of points first is the winner.

DID YOU KNOW?

In the Hawaiian Islands, people traditionally played with a stone disk instead of a ball.

The Line Game

Valverde del Fresno, Spain

- **Number of players:** 2 to 6
- **Material:** 3 flat stones or shoe heels for each player

1 A line about a foot long (31 cm) is drawn on the ground. The throwing line is marked at a distance of about 6½ feet (2 m).

2 A square of approximately 8 by 8 inches (20 by 20 cm) is drawn in the middle of the line.

3 Players take turns tossing their stones.

4 Scores are calculated depending on where and how the stone falls:
- if the the stone falls inside the square, the player earns 4 points;
- if the stone lands on a line, she earns 2 points;
- if the stone falls at closer than a hand's width from the line, she earns 1 point.

5 After 3 tosses, the winner is the player with the highest number of points.

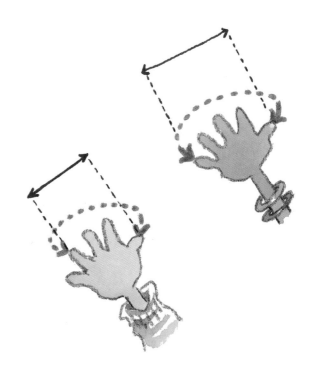

A hand's width can be measured in two different ways: using either four or five figures of one hand.

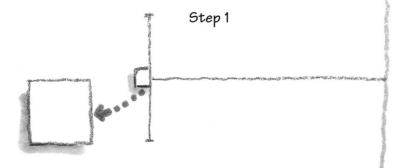

Step 1

Step 4

Button Soccer

Button soccer originated in Barcelona in 1940. The game can be played using buttons and a flat surface. Presently, there are several clubs that organize leagues.

Button Soccer

Cataluña and Valencia, Spain

Materials:

A table or a very even floor

The lines in the playing field are the same as a soccer field, with two more added to define the goal area.

The two goals may be made out of cardboard (for example, a shoebox with the proper dimensions).

Each team has 10 players on the field (buttons that represent players may be 1 to 1½ inches [2.5 to 4 cm] in diameter and a maximum of ½ inch [1 cm] high) and one button representing the goalkeeper (about 1½ inch [4 cm] in diameter and ½ inch [1.5 cm] high).

A small button that is flat on both sides represents the ball.

One button will be used as the kicker for each team.

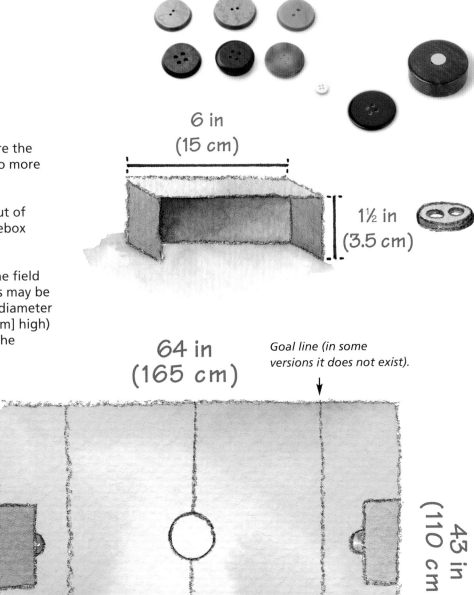

6 in
(15 cm)

1½ in
(3.5 cm)

64 in
(165 cm)

Goal line (in some versions it does not exist).

43 in
(110 cm)

How to play:

1 The teams are placed on the playing field as if they are playing a soccer game. The ball must be kicked out of the central circle at kick-off.

2 Each team moves one of its buttons.

3 When a button is ready to score, it must be located inside the opposite team's goal area. The player must also issue a warning of his intention to score. If he doesn't give a warning, the goal does not count.

4 To be counted, the button must completely cross the goal line.

5 After a team scores, all buttons return to their initial positions.

6 If a button touches another button from the opposite team but not the ball, it is considered a foul. If a foul occurs inside the penalty area, a penalty kick is awarded. The penalty follows the same rules as real soccer.

7 When a button leaves the field after touching the ball, it may go back in immediately but is not allowed to be moved in the next turn. The buttons leaving the playing field without having touched the ball may only go back when there is a foul, a score, or when the ball goes outside of the playing field.

8 The games have 2 periods of 15 minutes each and a 5-minute rest period. Every time the game is interrupted, the time lost is discounted.

9 The winner is the team with the higher score at the end of both periods.

To move a button, the player presses against the edge with the kicking button.

Home Again

In the games that follow, pieces always end up back at the starting point.

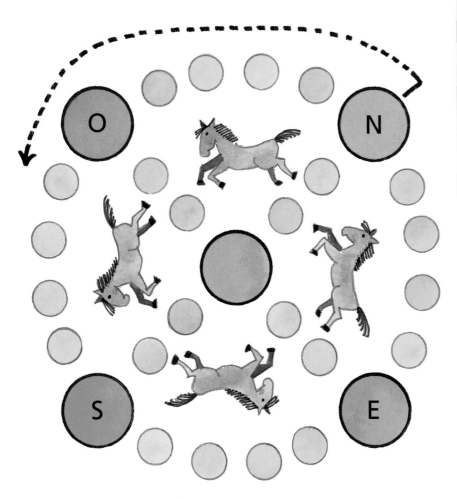

The illustration shows where the pieces enter to start.

Yut nori

Korea

- **Number of players:** 2 to 4
- **Material:** 4 dice with 2 sides and several playing pieces (the horses) for each player

Before the game begins, the pieces are distributed:
- 4 horses for each player if there are 2 players
- 3 horses for each player if there are 3 players
- 2 horses for each player if there are 4 players

1 The game starts with all the pieces off the board.

2 Each player takes turns throwing the four dice. A player moves his horses according to the number of sides he throws.

3 A player may have more than one horse on the board.

DID YOU KNOW?

Yut is a game traditionally played in Korea during the celebration of the New Year.

1 flat side:
A horse advances 1 position

2 flat sides:
A horse advances 2 positions

3 flat sides:
A horse advances 3 positions

4 flat sides:
A horse advances 4 positions and throws again

4 curved sides:
A horse advances 5 positions and throws again. With four flat sides or four curved sides, both scores may be added to move one horse or to advance two or more horses.

Step 4

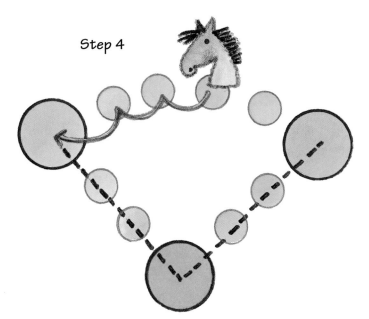

Step 6

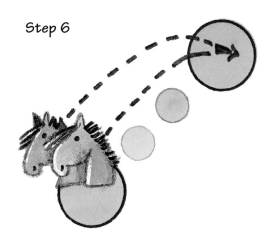

4 If a horse gets to the West, South, or East circle with an exact throw, it may continue on toward the center and then the North.

5 To force a horse off the board, an exact number must be tossed.

6 If 2 or more horses from the same player land in the same box, they may advance together with the next throw.

7 When a horse lands on a space occupied by an opponent, the opponent is eliminated and the player throws again. The eliminated player leaves the board and starts again at the North point.

8 The winner is the first player to get all his horses off the board.

Li'b el merafib

("The Hyena")

Played by the Baggara people in Sudan

- **Number of players:** 2 to 6
- **Material:** one piece for each player, one hyena piece, and 3 dice with 2 sides

1 Each player has a playing piece that represents her mother. She is to take her to the well for water while avoiding the hyena, who wants to eat her. Each space represents a trip that lasts a day.

2 All the mothers start at the village.

3 The dice represent different actions:
- 1 flat side up: the player gets to throw again;
- 2 flat sides up: 2 moves;
- 3 flat sides up: 3 moves and the player throws again;
- 3 rounded sides up: 6 moves and the player throws again.

4 A player must get one flat side up in order to move her mother out of the village.

5 When the mother has left the village, she moves along the spiral, advancing as many days as the dice indicate.

6 If the player gets another flat side up, she keeps it to be used later.

7 Each player keeps throwing until she gets a two (2 flat sides up).

Step 1

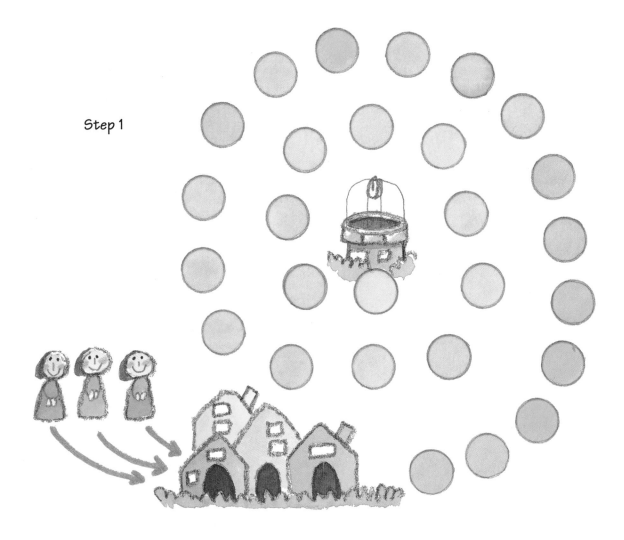

Step 3

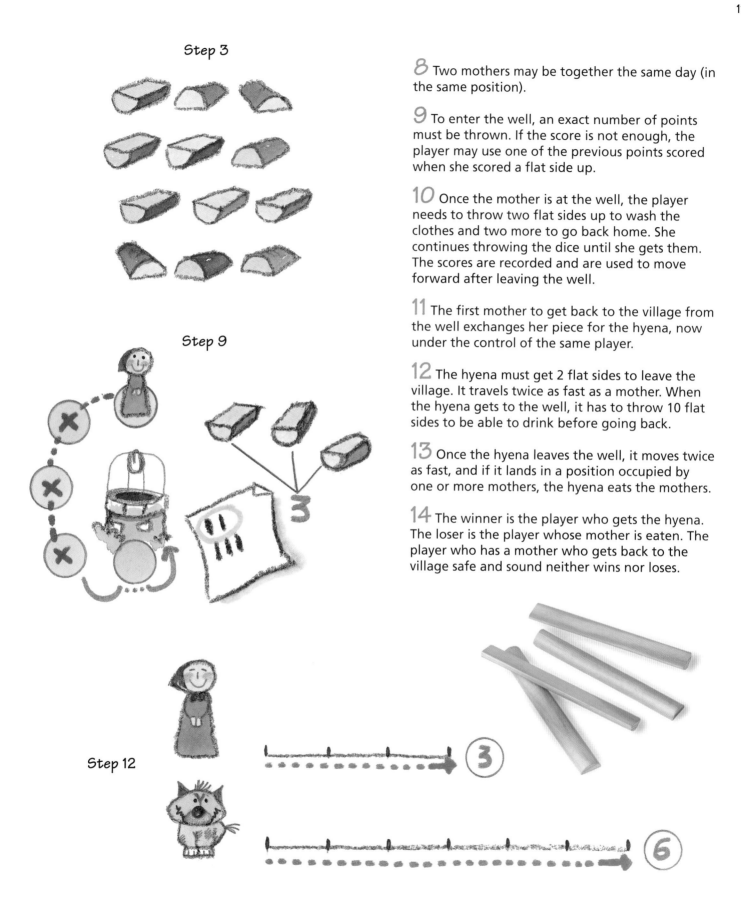

Step 9

Step 12

8 Two mothers may be together the same day (in the same position).

9 To enter the well, an exact number of points must be thrown. If the score is not enough, the player may use one of the previous points scored when she scored a flat side up.

10 Once the mother is at the well, the player needs to throw two flat sides up to wash the clothes and two more to go back home. She continues throwing the dice until she gets them. The scores are recorded and are used to move forward after leaving the well.

11 The first mother to get back to the village from the well exchanges her piece for the hyena, now under the control of the same player.

12 The hyena must get 2 flat sides to leave the village. It travels twice as fast as a mother. When the hyena gets to the well, it has to throw 10 flat sides to be able to drink before going back.

13 Once the hyena leaves the well, it moves twice as fast, and if it lands in a position occupied by one or more mothers, the hyena eats the mothers.

14 The winner is the player who gets the hyena. The loser is the player whose mother is eaten. The player who has a mother who gets back to the village safe and sound neither wins nor loses.

Index of Games by Continents

The world is full of boys and girls who know how to have fun playing games. Choose a game from any continent and try it. You are sure to find new ways to have fun and you will also discover how children who live thousands of miles away from you enjoy their play time.

NORTH AMERICA

SOUTH AMERICA

118

Boards for different games

The following pages give examples of game boards used to play the various games in this book. Photocopy them or use them as a guide to make your own . Don't forget to laminate your copy before you begin to play!

Game of alquerque, page 16

Solitaire, page 23

Surakarta, page 26

Checkerboard, page 34

Suag ma, page 58

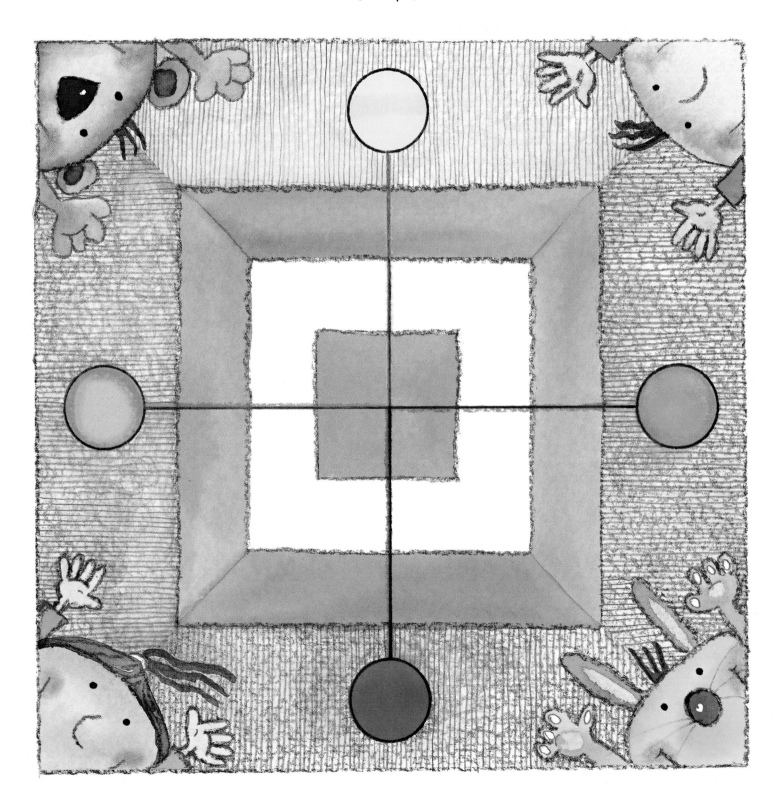

The Royal Game of Ur, page 59

Yut Nori, page 112